Jossey-Bass Teacher

Jossey-Bass Teacher provides K–12 teachers with essential knowledge and tools to create a positive and lifelong impact on student learning. Trusted and experienced educational mentors offer practical classroom-tested and theory-based teaching resources for improving teaching practice in a broad range of grade levels and subject areas. From one educator to another, we want to be your first source to make every day your best day in teaching. *Jossey-Bass Teacher* resources serve two types of informational needs—essential knowledge and essential tools.

Essential knowledge resources provide the foundation, strategies, and methods from which teachers may design curriculum and instruction to challenge and excite their students. Connecting theory to practice, essential knowledge books rely on a solid research base and time-tested methods, offering the best ideas and guidance from many of the most experienced and well-respected experts in the field.

Essential tools save teachers time and effort by offering proven, ready-to-use materials for in-class use. Our publications include activities, assessments, exercises, instruments, games, ready reference, and more. They enhance an entire course of study, a weekly lesson, or a daily plan. These essential tools provide insightful, practical, and comprehensive materials on topics that matter most to K–12 teachers.

JOSSEY-BASS
A Wiley Imprint
www.josseybass.com

Science Month by Month, Grades 3–8

Practical Ideas and Activities for Teachers and Homeschoolers

Julia Farish Spencer, Ph.D.

BICENTENNIAL
1807
WILEY
2007
BICENTENNIAL

John Wiley & Sons, Inc.

Published by Jossey-Bass
A Wiley Imprint
989 Market Street, San Francisco, CA 94103–1741   www.josseybass.com

Some material previously published as *The Science Teacher's Almanac* by Julia Spencer Moutran.

Jossey-Bass books and products are available through most bookstores. To contact Jossey-Bass directly call our Customer Care Department within the U.S. at 800-956-7739, outside the U.S. at 317-572-3986, or fax 317-572-4002.

Jossey-Bass also publishes its books in a variety of electronic formats. Some content that appears in print may not be available in electronic books.

ISBN-13: 978-0-471-72901-3
ISBN-10: 0-471-72901-9

Printed in the United States of America
FIRST EDITION
PB Printing   10 9 8 7 6 5 4 3 2 1

Contents

1. September

Introduce your students to the book and the monthly calendar. This month will encourage students to think scientifically, using their reasoning and imagination for exciting investigations.

2. October

Instead of an Oktoberfest, have a Science Fest and learn about science. This month includes National Health Day, so several health and nutrition activities are included. Learn about healthy tissue, the basic food groups, and how to use a microscope.

3. November

Go beyond our world into outer space. Since you and your students will find out about space milestones, let this be your month to investigate spacecraft, spacesuits, lunar rocks, and space foods.

4. December

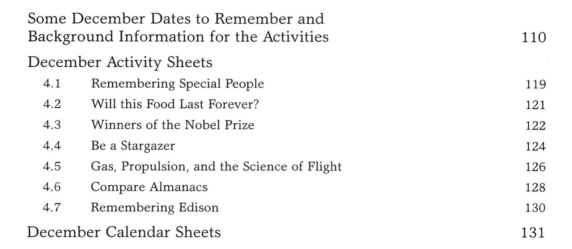

This is a month to remember others, including famous people who have made a difference in our world. It's a time to learn about the Nobel Prize winners.

5. January

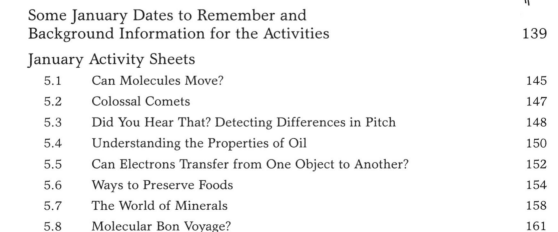

This is a month that "matters." Learn about molecules, electrons, atoms, electricity, science magic, sound, and rocks and minerals.

6. February

This is a natural month for learning about animals, including hibernators, cold-blooded animals (the earthworm), burrowers, and more. Create wildlife notebooks and "invent an invention."

7. March

There is never a better time to learn about plants, especially with dormant plants starting to bud and the coming of spring. Investigate the daffodil, apples, and clover.

8. April

April is Earth Month, so we learn more about protecting our planet in this chapter. Included are investigations on recycling, clean water, endangered species, wildlife and forest conservation, and activities for Arbor Day.

9. May–June

Here is a cumulative review of science milestones, including recognition of famous people and plans to help you design a school science project. Also learn about the summer solstice.

Appendixes

About This Book

Science Month by Month offers you science activities and background information for every month of the school year. You can easily use it at any time without complicated or elaborate planning.

For each month, you will find:

- *A blank monthly calendar.* This calendar can be enlarged and posted on the bulletin board, used for your lesson planning, or reproduced and given to students to fill in.
- *Dates to remember and background information for the activities.* This is a list of calendar events that deal with science and related historic events or landmarks. This section also provides some basic background information for the activities.
- *Activity sheets.* These reproducible activity sheets are correlated to many of the calendar dates. However, the activities may be done any time during the school year with your units of study without correlations to the dates.
- *Weekly calendar sheets.* The five calendar sheets at the end of each section can be used in various ways. They can be reproduced and given to your students so that they can write assignments on them. Or you can use them as lesson plan notes. You might even think of other ways in which to use them.

A special feature of this book is the appendixes. You'll find charts and forms, including a student progress chart, a science certificate, a biographical sketch form, and science vocabulary words. There are lists of recommended books, computer software, and videos and DVDs that correlate to the activities in this book. Students will learn science trivia each month by playing the trivia game in Appendix 5, with new game cards provided for each month. Answer keys for the activity sheets are also included.

Science Month by Month is correlated to the National Science Standards. Whatever science programs or books you currently use, *Science Month by Month* will complement and extend your students' learning, background information, and ability to think scientifically. You and your students will also have lots of fun!

To my children, Meredith and Melanie Moutran;
my sister, Lynn W. Spencer;
and my mother, Julia F. Spencer

About the Author

Julia Farish Spencer, Ph.D., received her bachelor of science degree from the University of Virginia and her master of arts degree and her doctorate from the University of Connecticut. She has taught science in grades 3 through 8 in the Knoxville, Tennessee, and West Hartford, Connecticut, public school systems. She was also an adjunct professor at the University of Connecticut in West Hartford.

Dr. Spencer is the president of Literary Workshops and Publications, a publisher and certified Connecticut continuing education unit that provides seminars and workshops for educators. She is a coproducer of the animated science narrative film *The Story of Punxsutawney Phil,* available from Phoenix Learning, and she reviews and correlates science videos with K–12 science texts.

Dr. Spencer is the author of fourteen science storybooks, including *The Story of Punxsutawney Phil, The Fearless Forecaster; Collecting Bugs and Things; Will Spring Ever Come to Gobbler's Knob?; G is for Groundhogs; My First Pet;* and *Punxsutawney Phil and His Weather Wisdom.*

September

September starts off with an annotated list of several important dates followed by activity sheets for many of the entries. You may want to recognize a particular event that occurred without doing an investigation or activity sheet. You may also want your students to read about an event and report to the class what they found out through their own research.

The information that follows is a brief overview to help you and your students with background information. You will want to consult other resources, including your science texts, for more specific information.

Some September Dates to Remember and Background Information for the Activities

Activity sheets are provided for starred dates only. It is your decision whether to give the students facts on each entry. And for the trivia game referred to, go to Appendix 5.

3* *Viking 2 landed on Mars (1976). Viking 2* found proof of a past watery environment on Mars. Introduce your students to the fascinating facts about this planet—its canyons, channels, lava plains, and different seasons. See Activity Sheet 1.1.

A day on Mars is 24.5 hours in Earth time; a year is 687 days. Called the "red planet," Mars rotates on an axis similar to Earth's. Through space exploration, like the *Mars Global Surveyor, Pathfinder,* and *Mars Odyssey,* we have learned much about this neighboring planet. This is a great time to encourage your students to think scientifically. Have them read and find out about Mars and imagine what the planet is like, especially its seasons. Activity Sheet 1.1 encourages students to think about Earth and its seasons, as well as what seasons might be like on another planet.

4 *Power Day in New York.* On this day in 1882, Thomas Edison and his electric power company officially opened its first electric power station on Pearl Street in Manhattan, making New York the first city to have city-wide electricity.

9* *California Admission Day.* The state of California was admitted to the Union on this date in 1850. This is an opportunity to recognize California as one of our largest states, in both area and population. California leads the United States in agricultural production, growing many important food products such as the avocado.

Avocados were first planted in California in the mid-1800s. They are an important crop and are very nutritious. Activity Sheet 1.2 will help students learn first-hand about growing plants from seeds, transplanting plants, and recording their observations systematically. Have students learn about California's geography and products by visiting the home page Web site: www.ca.gov/state/portal/myca_home page.jsp. (This is the first of several states students will encounter in this book.)

9 *Birthday of Luigi Galvani (1737).* Galvani was an Italian physicist and physician. He realized that animal muscle tissue had electricity as he observed and experimented with frogs' legs. His research influenced his contemporaries, such as Alessandro Volta, who created the first battery (the "voltaic pile"). The galvanometer, an instrument used to detect or measure a small electric current, was named in honor of Galvani. Volta proved that Galvani's theory was incorrect. He showed the frog's tissue was carrying an electric current between two metals.

10* *Elias Howe received a patent for the sewing machine (1846).* Where would we be without this important invention? This is a perfect time to introduce your students to the importance of science in the development of machines and other inventions.

Each year, thousands of people apply for and receive patents for their inventions. Introduce the students to the *World Almanac,* which lists the patents awarded each year.

Help students understand that a patent is an award—a grant and license given to someone for the exclusive use, sale, and distribution of his or her claimed invention. It is a legal protection. More than ninety thousand patents are distributed each year. Visit the U.S. Patent Web site at www.uspto.gov for information on patents. Let your students create an invention and describe it on Activity Sheet 1.3.

11 *First operation of hydroelectric generator at Hoover Dam.* In 1936, Hoover Dam sent power over 300 miles from the Colorado River in Nevada to Los Angeles, California. The dam stands 726 feet high and is 1,233 feet long. Encourage your students to find a picture of Hoover Dam in library books.

13* *Birthday of Walter Reed (1851).* This American pathologist is best remembered for his work in Cuba, where he helped identify the cause of yellow fever. Reed and his associates found that a mosquito was the carrier of this deadly disease, which infected many people.

This is an opportunity to find out about the anatomy of a mosquito and how it actually "bites" a person or an animal. Being aware of the feeding patterns of mosquitoes and ways to prevent getting bitten by them (they seldom feed in the middle of the day) is education for all. (See Activity Sheet 1.4.) Also, discuss any current events regarding mosquitoes and their nature, available through your newspapers, if appropriate, or Web sites. Updates on the West Nile virus can be found on the California state Web site: www.ca.gov/state/portal/myca_homepage.jsp.

13* *World's highest recorded temperature (Africa, 1922).* This is a good time to talk about seasonal differences around the world and temperature ranges (recording high and low temperatures). You may want to record your area's temperatures for a week and compare them to a previous year's statistics for the same dates.

Activity Sheet 1.5 helps students compute a mathematical average. It also helps them record important weather statistics. (September's trivia game in Appendix 5 reveals the recorded high temperature.)

14 *Birthday of Ivan Pavlov (1849).* This famous Russian received a Nobel Prize for his study of the physiology of animals and the structure of the brain and its relationship to nerves and muscles. (See the December entry and teacher information on the Nobel Prize.) He trained a dog to salivate on command, using a bell to teach the dog to associate food with a sound. Pavlov left a valuable legacy for science research. Many future scientists built on his findings in animal behavior and learning.

15* *Birthday of Frank Eugene Lutz (1879).* This famous American entomologist, educator, and museum curator was the first curator of the Department of Entomology at the American Museum of Natural History in New York. He established America's first guided nature trail in Harriman State Park, New York. As a young man, he was fascinated with insects and the process of metamorphosis, and he created insect dioramas.

In honor of Lutz, have students complete the chart on insect communication in Activity Sheet 1.6.

You may want them to work in small groups on completing the chart, and they could make a poster on insect communication and hang the posters in the classroom. You may also want to temporarily bring some insects into the classroom using bug cages, but only if the students have researched and safely caught the insect and plan to return it to its natural environment. Of course, for safety reasons, preapprove which insects may be observed, such as a cricket.

A visit to your local museum where insects are displayed may be an added benefit. Students can research insects online or in the library. The list of science books and literature in Appendix 2 can be used as a reference, but students should be encouraged to find their own more extensive and age-appropriate references by utilizing multiple resources.

Finally, talk to the students about seasonal autumn changes for insects, such as the migration of monarch butterflies and crickets laying their eggs. Since this is September, many insects are preparing for winter in certain climates, and for some, the last rite is the laying of eggs, which will usually hatch the following spring or summer.

18* *Birthday of Jean Foucalt, French physicist (1819).* Foucalt invented a method for measuring the speed of light. The experiment he devised was performed entirely within the laboratory. Foucalt found that the path of a light beam may be bent when it encounters an obstacle.

Activity Sheet 1.7 gives your students a chance to investigate what happens to light as it passes through water.

19* *Birthday of George Cadbury, English manufacturer (1839).* Cadbury chocolates are famous and enjoyed worldwide for their excellent quality and delicious taste. Chocolate has its own tale to tell. The production begins with the cacao tree, grown in regions near the equator, such as Africa, Indonesia, and South America.

The tree produces a fruit the size of a pineapple, ripe with cocoa beans. The beans are fermented, dried, and roasted. Then the nib or meat of the bean is extracted in a process called *winnowing.*

Have students visit the Cadbury Web site at www.cadbury.co.uk. They can learn about the history of chocolate and how it is made, and how the cacao tree is harvested. For nutritional purposes, they can read the list of ingredients on chocolate bars or on Cadbury chocolate eggs.

Cadbury's food processing techniques were scientific and as one of the first food processors to use scientific food processing techniques, this helped create a standard for federal legislation for good safety and guidelines for food manufacturing.

Have students research and find other food manufacturing sites for chocolate, such as www.hersheys.com. Here they can go on a virtual tour of the production of chocolate, from the trees used in production, to the dairy farms, to the final products. There is also a teacher site at www.hersheys.com to support this classroom lesson.

Students can complete Activity Sheet 1.8.

22* *Birthday of Michael Faraday, English chemist (1791).* Faraday contributed much to our knowledge of magnetism and electricity. He found that an electric current could be induced in a coil of wire when a permanent magnet is moved in and out of a wire coil. His work with electromagnets led to his law of electromagnetic induction.

Help your students discover these facts about magnets: magnets exist in natural and manu-factured forms; lodestone, a natural mag-net, is a rock containing iron; and manufactured magnets attract iron and other metals and are frequently made of steel or iron.

Magnets have two ends called *poles.* Opposite poles attract; similar poles repel. The magnet operates in a field of energy called a *magnetic field.* Lines of force are observable between the ends of the magnets, where the greatest strength is found. Larger, more powerful magnets have broader and wider lines of force. (See Activity Sheet 1.9.)

20–23 *First day of fall, the autumnal equinox.* On the day of the equinox, which takes place between September 20 and 23, depending on the year, the sun crosses the celestial equator, and day and night are everywhere

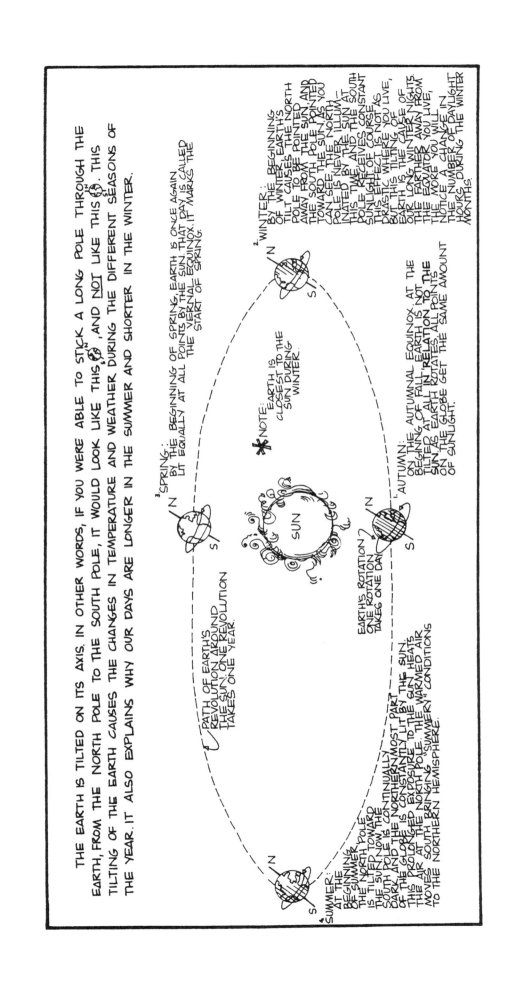

of equal length. After the autumnal equinox, Earth's tilt on its axis means that more of the sun's rays are directed at the Southern Hemisphere, so the hours of daylight decrease and hours of darkness increase in the Northern Hemisphere, and there is warm weather in the Southern Hemisphere and cool weather in the Northern Hemisphere.

Have your students draw pictures of the sun and Earth during the four seasons. Shade half of Earth in darkness. Have the students label the North and South Poles and the equator, as shown in the illustration.

24* *Birthday of Howard Florey, Australian-English pathologist (1898).* Penicillin was discovered in 1928 by Sir Alexander Fleming. Following his discovery, two other scientists, Howard Florey and Ernst Chain, isolated the drug and purified it for clinical use. All three men were awarded the coveted Nobel Prize. (See "Some December Dates to Remember" in Chapter Four.)

These advances in medicine have helped cut death rates from some infectious diseases. Penicillin is an antibiotic that works to destroy harmful bacteria.

Fleming discovered penicillin in common mold. He found that certain conditions encourage the growth of mold and certain conditions retard its growth. Help your students discover some of these conditions by doing the investigation provided in Activity 1.10.

You may also want to invite a pharmacist, physician, or school nurse to talk to the students about penicillin as a helpful drug. Also discuss the precautions in taking it and in storing it.

26 *Birthday of Archibald Hill, English physiologist (1886).* This is an opportunity to recognize the contributions of another Nobel Prize winner. Hill, who won the prize in 1922, was a biophysicist and physiologist who experimented with frogs and their nerve and muscle tissues. He discovered the importance of oxygen as a gas to the functions of the body, including its role in the relaxation and recovery phases of muscular contractions. Like Galvani and Pavlov, Hill's extensive experimentation contributed to our understanding of physiology.

Although no activity is provided in conjunction with Hill, you may want to observe and talk about tadpoles and frogs and their physiology. There are computer-generated frog dissection programs available for purchase through science materials catalogues such as the biological supply company listed in Appendix 2.

30* *Birthday of Hans Geiger, German physicist (1882).* Geiger is known for his study of the atom and the invention of the Geiger counter, an instrument used to measure particles of radiation. Geiger found and identified the *alpha particle* as the nucleus of the helium atom. Like Edison and Faraday, his research was based on an understanding of the principles of magnetism, electricity, and the nature of the atom.

Here is an illustration of an atom. In the center is the nucleus, containing protons and neutrons. Orbiting around it are electrons.

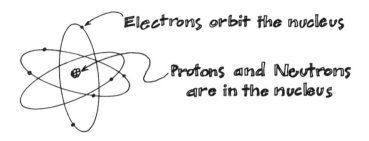

Electrons orbit the nucleus

Protons and Neutrons are in the nucleus

Protons and neutrons do not leave the atom, but electrons can. They can "hop" or move to another atom.

Geiger studied the composition of atoms, particularly helium atoms. You may want to have your students read about atoms, electricity, or helium. You may also want to introduce them to the Periodic Table.

Electricity, the study of the movement of electrons of atoms in different patterns, is investigated in the recommended activity for this date. If electrons move in the same direction or pattern, we call this *DC,* or *direct current.* If they move in different directions, we call that *AC,* or *alternating current.*

Batteries use conductors to carry the electrons. Batteries are used to start electric currents. They make electrons flow in a certain path or direct current. Sometimes copper is used as a conductor, as it was in the first battery, created by Volta. (See the September 9 entry for Luigi Galvani.)

TERMINALS

9 VOLT

SUPER HEAVY DUTY BATTERY

NEVER DIE

Batteries are measured in volts. In the investigation using Activity Sheet 1.11, have your students observe the path or circuit of electrons by using a battery to illuminate a lightbulb.

Activity Sheet 1.1.

What Would the Fall Season Be Like on Mars?

On Earth, the fall season is different from the summer, spring, and winter seasons. There are changes in weather, the temperature, the growth of plants, the habits of animals, and the color of leaves in some trees. Think of all the changes that occur in the fall on Earth.

Now read about Mars and its seasons. Does the temperature change on that planet? Do the volcanoes, ice caps, and atmosphere change? Where is the planet in relation to the sun?

Use your imagination and some information you learn from your investigation to describe fall on Mars. Use the report form here to write your story. Be sure to include any interesting facts you learn about Mars. Remember there are science facts and there is science fiction, which is the art of embellishing the facts for the story. Then draw some pictures of Mars and share the story and sketches with your teacher and friends.

Visit these Web sites to tour Mars: www.mars.jpl.asa.gov/mgs and www.nineplanets.org/mars.html.

What Would the Fall Season Be Like on Mars? *(Cont'd.)*

Activity Sheet 1.2.

Celebrate California and the Avocado Tree

Materials

plastic container or glass jar

3 wooden toothpicks

avocado seed

water

potting soil

large pot

small shovel

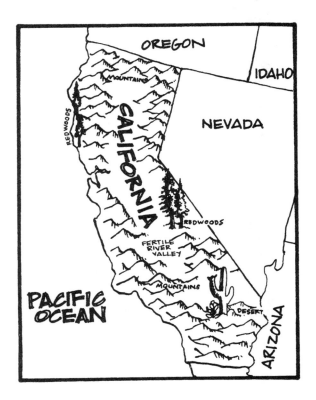

Procedure

1. Fill the container or glass jar three-quarters full of water. Push the three toothpicks into the avocado seed so that the toothpicks hold half of the seed out of the water. The seed should look like the illustration, with the toothpicks supporting it.

2. Keep the water level touching about ¼ inch of the seed at all times. Give the seed sunlight; place it on a windowsill.

Celebrate California and
the Avocado Tree *(Cont'd.)*

3. Observe the roots as they appear on the seed. When a stem and leaves appear, transplant the growing seed to a large pot with soil.

4. Observe the growth of the tree.

Option: Cut off part of the pointed end of the seed before putting the toothpicks into it. See if the seed grows faster. The wider, broad end should face downward.

Conclusion

Complete the chart to show the dates and sketches of your avocado seed.

For more information, visit www.dre.ca.gov/gardening.htm.

Date of original rooting: _____   Date of transplant: _____

	description:	sketch:
1st observation date:	description:	sketch:
2nd observation date:	description:	sketch:
3rd observation date:	description:	sketch:
4th observation date:	description:	sketch:
5th observation date:	description:	sketch:

Activity Sheet 1.3.

Patent an Invention

Think about an invention you could make that might be patented. Use the form with this activity sheet to illustrate your invention and describe its purpose and use. You don't have to invent it, but you have to use your imagination and creativity and apply for your patent. Then your teacher will sign your patent award, shown below, for your success and discovery.

For example, in order to prevent burning buildings from collapsing too quickly, a new patent was issued for an invention of hollow beams filled with water and steam. Using these hollow beams in a building's infrastructure will minimize a potential fire's heat and slow damage, thus helping to prevent a building from collapsing. The patent number is 6,763,645, and you can visit the Web site of the U.S. Patent Office at www.uspto.gov for information.

More than 1.7 million U.S. patents have been issued since 1975. The *World Almanac* lists all major inventions and discoveries, including new finds in biology, physics, and chemistry, by nation, year, inventor, and invention. Read the almanac in your library or online at www.worldalmanacforkids.com. See if you can find when the Geiger counter was invented.

Patent no. _____

awarded to _____

for _____

_____

date _____   *signed* _____

Name: _____   **Date:** _____

Write a description of your invention on the lines provided. Then draw a picture

of your invention in the space on the table. Draw your face in the space provided.

_____
Patent Number

_____
Name of Invention

16

Activity Sheet 1.4.

What Do You Know About Mosquitoes?

Do you know how a mosquito "bites"? In fact, it pierces (rather than bites) the skin with its sharp stylets that are attached to a long, thin tube called a *proboscis*. Within half a minute, the female mosquito is able to reach one of your blood vessels and withdraw blood that she needs to complete her egg production process. During the time her stylets are piercing and withdrawing blood, she injects a saliva fluid that temporarily keeps your blood from coagulating or clotting. The male mosquito feeds on plants and does not pierce the skin at all.

Using the diagram, complete the chart below. Label the body parts of the mosquito. Then try to find out how many species of mosquitoes exist.

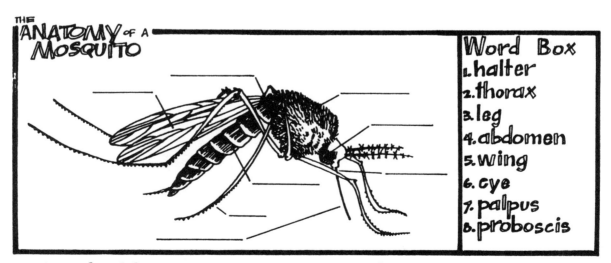

THE **ANATOMY** OF A **MOSQUITO**

Word Box
1. halter
2. thorax
3. leg
4. abdomen
5. wing
6. eye
7. palpus
8. proboscis

Fill in the blanks with words from the word box.

17

Name _____   Date _____

Activity Sheet 1.5.

Averaging Weather Temperatures

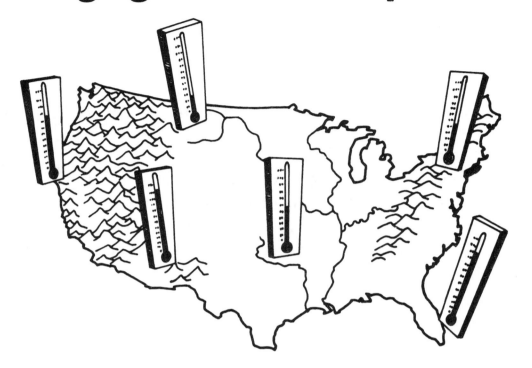

Make four copies of the chart on this activity sheet, and use it to record the high and low temperatures for four cities in different parts of the country for four days. Then average the high temperatures and the low temperatures for those four days. To take a statistical average, follow the example here:

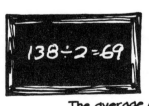

The average of 78 and 60 is 69.

The average temperature in Boston on September 1 was 69°

Averaging Weather Temperatures *(Cont'd.)*

You need four copies of this chart. For each city, color in each column up to the line that marks the day's high and low temperatures. Then calculate the average temperature for each day.

CITY NAME

TEMPERATURE (°F)

| 100 |
| 90 |
| 80 |
| 70 |
| 60 |
| 50 |
| 40 |
| 30 |
| 20 |
| 10 |
| 0 |
| -10 |
| -20 |

HIGH LOW HIGH LOW HIGH LOW HIGH LOW

Day 1   Day 2   Day 3   Day 4

DATE   DATE   DATE   DATE

Average temperature
Day 1 _____

Average temperature
Day 2 _____

Average temperature
Day 3 _____

Average temperature
Day 4 _____

19

Name _____   Date _____

How Do Insects Communicate?

There are many kinds or species of insects that communicate or talk to each other. Some communicate by visual signal. Have you ever seen a firefly "flash"? Some communicate by sound. Have you ever heard a cricket "chirp"? Other insects communicate by releasing chemicals called *pheromones* to attract their mates. Did you know that moths do this? Also, some insects communicate by activity or movement. Have you seen a worker honey bee perform a "round dance" telling the other bees where the food is located?

Research insects and how they communicate by reading books on insects or reading sources on the Internet that provide valuable information regarding insect communication. Then complete the chart here: list three insects in each category, briefly explaining how they communicate.

"Science Fluency"

Look us up:

Entomology
Entomologist
Pheromones

Definitions: (Write a definition for each word.)

Entomology: _____

_____

_____

Entomologist: _____

_____

_____

Pheromones: _____

_____

_____

20

How Do Insects Communicate? *(Cont'd.)*

In each column, list three insects and how they communicate.

Insects that use visual signals	Insects that use sound	Insects that use chemicals	Insects that use movement
1.	1.	1.	1.
2.	2.	2.	2.
3.	3.	3.	3.

Activity Sheet 1.7.

Can the Path of Light Be Bent?

In this activity, you will see how light appears to bend in the process called refraction.

Materials

hammer

small nail

empty coffee can with one end removed

2 or 3 sheets of $8\frac{1}{2} \times 11$ black construction paper

masking tape

$1\frac{1}{2}$ cups of water

2-cup glass measuring cup

1 sheet of white construction paper or oak tag

flashlight

felt-tip marker

Procedure

1. Using the hammer and nail, make a tiny hole in the bottom of the coffee can. (**Caution:** Be careful when working with the hammer and nail, and look out for sharp edges around the nail hole.)

2. Completely cover the coffee can with black construction paper. Leave an opening for the pinhole on the bottom. Leave the other end open to insert the flashlight.

3. Lay the covered coffee can on its side on another sheet of black paper. Tape the can to the paper to keep it from rolling. Angle the can so that the pinhole is aimed at the measuring cup.

4. Fill the measuring cup with $1\frac{1}{2}$ cups of water. Put the cup on top of and in the center of a sheet of white paper.

Can the Path of Light Be Bent? *(Cont'd.)*

5. Completely darken the room. (It must be *absolutely* dark.) Turn on the flashlight, and aim it through the pinhole in the coffee can to the middle of the measuring cup.

6. Look at the path of the light. What happens when it reaches the cup of water?

7. Take your marker, and trace the path on the white paper. What is the direction once it hits water?

WHEN LIGHT PASSES THROUGH WATER, **REFRACTION** CHANGES THE ANGLE OF THE LIGHTWAVE SLIGHTLY. THAT'S WHY WHEN YOU LOOK AT SOMEONE STANDING IN WATER, THE PART OUT OF THE WATER DOESN'T SEEM TO MATCH WITH THE PART IN THE WATER.

Conclusions

1. What did the path of light do once it hit the water?

2. Look up the word *refraction*. You may want to consult a science dictionary or look online for a reference dictionary to define it. What does it mean? Record the definition on your vocabulary form.

3. Can you make any science predictions regarding the angle of the light wave? Explain them on the back of this paper.

Activity Sheet 1.8.

The Story of Chocolate, an Amazing Journey

We have delicious chocolate to eat thanks to families like the Hersheys in the United States and the Cadburys in England.

Did you ever wonder how chocolate is made? It starts with the growth of the cacao tree seedling and ends with the candy bar you buy. There are many steps along the way, which you can discover online. Visit the Cadbury Web site at www.cadbury.co.uk and www.cadburylearningzone.co.uk or the Hershey Web site at www.hersheys.com, and follow the amazing journey of chocolate, from the seedling to the finished product.

Then use the information you learned to unscramble the following pictures of the production of chocolate and correctly number them from 1 to 7. Write the numeral 1 under the first picture in the amazing journey of chocolate, and follow the same process numbering the rest.

The Story of Chocolate, an Amazing Journey *(Cont'd.)*

On the line beneath the picture, correctly number the pictures from numeral 1 to numeral 7, as they occur in the production of chocolate.

_____

_____

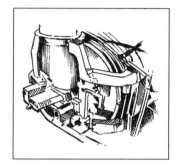

_____

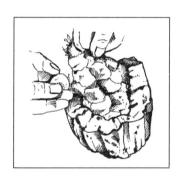

_____

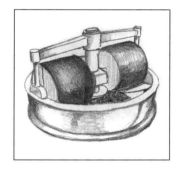

_____

_____

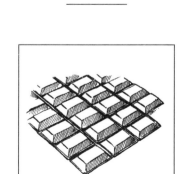

_____

The Story of Chocolate, an Amazing Journey *(Cont'd.)*

"Science Fluency"

Look us up:

Fermentation
Winnowing
Nib
Conching

Definitions: (Write a definition for each word.)

Fermentation:_____
_____
_____

Winnowing:_____
_____
_____

Nib: _____
_____
_____

Conching:_____
_____
_____

Activity Sheet 1.9.

Observing Magnetic Lines of Force

Materials

iron filings

paper or oak tag

4 bar magnets

nail

Procedure

1. Sprinkle some iron filings on a piece of paper or oak tag. You may need two people to hold the paper.

2. Beneath the paper, experiment with the bar magnets. Start by holding one bar magnet under the paper. What happens to the filings?

3. Next, put two magnets under the paper. Put their like poles together. What happens to the filings?

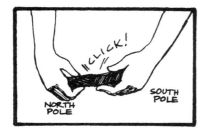  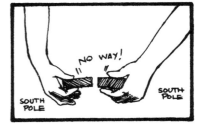

Observing Magnetic Lines of Force *(Cont'd.)*

4. Now put the two magnets under the paper. Put their opposite poles together. What happens to the filings? Pull the ends farther apart. What is the pattern of the filings as you separate the ends?

5. Take the nail, and hold it above the filings on top of the paper. The magnet should not be near the nail.

6. Next, take the nail and hold it beneath the magnet on top of the filings as shown in the illustration.

7. What happens to the filings? Separate the magnet from the nail slowly by raising it higher in the air. What happens to the filings now?

Observing Magnetic Lines of Force *(Cont'd.)*

Conclusions

1. Draw sketches of the lines of force for the like poles.

2. Draw sketches of the lines of force for the unlike poles.

3. Draw a sketch of the lines of force for the single magnet.

4. Was the nail able to act as a magnet at any time? Look up the term *temporary magnet* in a book on magnetism. Did the nail become a temporary magnet?

To understand more and witness an animation of an electric generator at work, visit this Web site: www.sciencejoywagon.com/physicszone/lesson/otherpub/wfendt/generatorengl.htm.

Two other great Web sites are: www.wvic.com/how-gen-works.htm and www.amasei.com/amateur/coilgen.htm.

Name _____   Date _____

Activity Sheet 1.10.

Understanding Mold

In this activity, you will have the chance to learn about mold, a fuzzy material that often grows on plant or animal matter that is often damp or decaying.

Materials

6 empty baby food jars with lids

1 household sponge cut into 3 squares to fit the bottoms of 3 jars

water

scissors

3 bread rolls made without preservatives

pencil and paper to make labels

tongs

cellophane tape

plastic bag and twist-tie

> **Warning:** Adult supervision required. Students with asthma or mold allergy should not participate.

Procedure

1. Put the three cut sponges in the bottom of three baby food jars.
2. Dampen the sponges with water until they are wet but not soaking.
3. Divide the three rolls into six equal parts—one for each jar. Put three pieces on top of the three wet sponges in the three baby food jars. Put the other three pieces of rolls into the remaining three baby food jars. Put the lids on top of all six jars.

Understanding Mold *(Cont'd.)*

4. Make labels for the six jars to indicate locations of the investigation: one dark area (under the cabinet or in the closet), one sunny area (near the window), and one cool area (in an ice bucket or in the refrigerator but not the freezer). Tape the labels to the six jars. The jars will be placed in pairs, two jars in each of the three locations—one with a sponge and one without a sponge. Tape the labels to the jars.

5. Observe the jars for the next week. Look at the six jars every day and return them after observation. Record your results on the Mold Observation Chart.

6. After completing the chart on the last day, remove the bread from each jar, using tongs if necessary. Observe the growth and appearance of the molds. Place the bread and the sponges in a plastic bag, and tie it for your teacher to discard.

Conclusions

1. Complete the Mold Observation Chart.
2. What conditions encouraged the most growth of mold?

Mold Observation Chart

Jar 6
COOL AREA, WITH SPONGE

Jar 5
COOL AREA, NO SPONGE

Jar 4
SUNNY AREA, WITH SPONGE

Jar 3
SUNNY AREA, NO SPONGE

Jar 2
DARK AREA, WITH SPONGE

Jar 1
DARK AREA, NO SPONGE

Day 5 Day 4 Day 3 Day 2 Day 1

Activity Sheet 1.11.

What Makes a Complete Circuit?

Materials

1 6-volt dry cell battery

1 small (3.5 to 6 volts) flashlight bulb

1 lightbulb holder, sized to fit lightbulb

scissors or wire cutters

2 1-foot pieces of coated flex wire

screwdriver

Procedure

1. Place the dry cell battery on a table. Examine the two terminals. Do they look alike?

2. Screw the small lightbulb into the lightbulb holder.

3. Use scissors or wire cutters to carefully strip the ends (remove the protective coating) from the flex wire so that the wire is exposed about 1 inch on each end.

4. Attach the ends of the two wires to the battery terminals and the lightbulb holder terminals. Use the screwdriver to unscrew the screws on the lightbulb holder. Once the wires are connected, tighten the lightbulb holder screws to secure the wire.

   An optional choice for connecting is available for viewing at http://www.dl.ket.org/physics/companion/thepc/compan/current/index.htm.

What Makes a Complete Circuit? *(Cont'd.)*

Conclusions

1. Why did you strip the coating from the wires?

2. What happens to the lightbulb when the wires are connected to the battery terminal and the lightbulb holder?

3. What happens to the light?

4. How does the battery help the electrons move? Do the electrons follow a certain path? Do they go in the same direction?

SEPTEMBER

1

2

3 *Viking 2* landed on Mars in 1976. Write a story about Autumn on Mars on Activity Sheet 1.1 and visit the Mars Web sites.

4 Guess which city was the first in America to have electric lights back in 1882? Play September trivia to find the answer. Your teacher will introduce you to the trivia game cards. Practice energy conservation at home by turning off unnecessary lights.

5

6

SEPTEMBER

7

Your teacher will show you how to use the Science Vocabulary List and your Mini-Report Form during this week.

8

9

Name the large western state that celebrates its statehood today. Then plant and observe the growth of an avocado seed by using Activity Sheet 1.2. Visit the state Web site and write a Mini-Report on this special state.

10

A very important machine was patented by Elias Howe in 1846 on this day. What is that machine? Play the trivia game to find out. Then do Activity Sheet 1.3.

11

This famous dam operated its first hydrolelectric generator in 1936. What is the name of the dam? Play the trivia game to find out. Can you find a picture of this dam in your library or on the Internet? Look for resource books or with a search engine under the name of the dam.

12

In 1959, the first spacecraft from Earth landed on the moon. To find out the name of this Soviet spacecraft, play the trivia game. Think: Where is Earth in its yearly orbit around the sun? While Earth rotates on its axis, what does the moon do?

Mt. Shasta (14,162 Feet)

San Francisco

Los Angeles

36

SEPTEMBER

13 Today we're going to learn about mosquitoes using Activity Sheet 1.4. Or, you may choose to make a weather chart using Activity Sheet 1.5. Did you know the hottest day ever was recorded in northern Africa on this date in 1922? How hot did it get? Play September trivia to find out.

14 If you have a dog, teach him a trick or give him a treat in honor of Ivan Pavlov. Your teacher will tell you a few facts about this scientist born on this day in 1849. You may want to record a few facts on your Biography Sketch form.

15 Today, we will learn how and why insects communicate using Activity Sheet 1.6. Why do fireflies flash and crickets chirp? Who was Frank Eugene Lutz? What is "entomology"?

16

17

18 Today you will experiment with light using Activity Sheet 1.7. What is *refraction*? Write its definition on your Vocabulary List.

37

SEPTEMBER

19 Celebrate the birthday of George Cadbury (1839). Learn how his manufacturing of chocolate makes chocolate so creamy. Go on an amazing chocolate journey using Activity Sheet 1.8.

20 Autumn officially begins this week with the arrival of the equinox. On this day, day and night on Earth are equal in length. Draw a picture of Earth and the sun on this day.

21

22 Learn about magnetism today using Activity Sheet 1.9.

23

24 Let's investigate mold today using Activity Sheet 1.10.

SEPTEMBER

25

26 Your teacher will tell you about a famous scientist named Archibald Hill. He was born on this date in 1886. Who was he?

27

28

29

30 Play September trivia game to find out about Hans Geiger. Then light a bulb by using Activity Sheet 1.11.

October

There are many interesting events to share with your students in October and eleven exciting activity sheets to highlight certain days of the month. Feel free to use the activity sheets in this chapter at any time of the year according to your curriculum and program of study. If you use them on the recommended dates, you and your class can celebrate important dates in the history of science.

Recognize the dedication and pursuit of goals and dreams of famous people highlighted this month—people like Louis-Antoine Ranvier, Thomas Edison, Antoni van Leeuwenhoek, William Morton, and Christopher Columbus. Although their pursuits were in different areas and their marks in history and science occurred at different times, their contributions will last forever. Depending on your students' grade level, mention the scientists' names and discoveries if they fit into your curriculum. Or you might choose to expand the curriculum to encompass these individuals to your students.

A brief summary of certain events is provided for your background information. For further information, consult science textbooks and other reference materials.

Some October Dates to Remember and Background Information for the Activities

Activity sheets are provided for starred dates only. It is your decision whether to give the students facts on each entry. And for the trivia game referred to, go to Appendix 5.

First Monday in October* *National Child Health Day.* In recognition of this day, a maze is provided in Activity Sheet 2.1. It focuses on good nutrition and regular exercise as ways to stay healthy. The activity is a fun food maze that students solve by making the wise food choices. Have students visit this Web site for facts about good nutrition: childdevelopmentinfo. com/health-safety/nutrition.shtm/.

Second Week in October* *Fire Prevention Week.* During this week, you may want to invite local firefighters to your school to talk to the students about fire prevention and safety precautions they can take in their homes.

During this time, you can tell students about the Great Chicago Fire of October 8, 1871. There is some dispute about the origin of the fire. Some historical sources claim that a cow living in a barn on Mrs. O'Leary's property kicked over an oil lantern inside the barn. The fire reportedly began there and continued to spread, claiming over two hundred lives and burning more than twenty-one hundred acres.

Other writers claim it was not the fault of the cow at all, but suggested that a comet caused the fire. There were similar fires that occurred that same evening in Wisconsin and Michigan at the same hour. (See the Books section in Appendix 2 for recommended reading for older students. You can find additional references to this story online that would be interesting to share with your class.)

Be sure to stress to children that fire is not always destructive; it can also be helpful. Fire is useful in cooking, giving warmth, and providing light. Ask how many students have enjoyed a campfire or sat by their glowing fireplace at home.

Control of fire is an important concept for students to understand. For Activity Sheet 2.2, students will learn about what a fire needs in order to burn. Talk to the students about the ways fire engines have improved since the steam fire engines used to extinguish the 1871 Chicago Fire (or have the firefighters address this progress when they visit your school).

Second Sunday in October* *School Lunch Week.* Activity Sheet 2.3 can be done at any time of the year, but it is especially beneficial during School Lunch Week. It provides a chart of the basic food groups and a crossword puzzle. (In 2005, the "food guide pyramid" was introduced.)

During this week, you may want to work with your school dietitian to allow students to plan the school's lunches for the week. This may have to be arranged several weeks in advance, as menus are often determined and printed early.

Your students may want to plan some meals at home too. They may also want to pay attention to their own eating habits to see if they are eating the recommended daily servings from the basic food groups.

If the school dietitian allows the students to plan the menu, perhaps they can host a luncheon in the cafeteria, planning centerpieces for the tables, making posters for the school hallways (about the menu and the food groups), and inviting special guests. Getting students involved in making choices about wise nutrition is beneficial for all.

Since Halloween is celebrated this month and pumpkins are ready to be harvested, a special pumpkin recipe is provided on the activity sheet. Bake some pumpkin bread with your students for all of you to enjoy together!

2* *French pathologist and histologist Louis-Antoine Ranvier was born (1835).* Ranvier became professor of general anatomy at the College of France in Paris. His students would flock to his lab to learn more from this brilliant scientist. He is particularly famous for his investigations and explorations of the nervous system, especially the structure and composition of nerves and their terminals. "Ranvier's tactile disks" is the name given to the nerve fibers connecting the epithelial cells on the tongue.

An investigation is given in Activity Sheet 2.4 to honor this scientist of the nineteenth century. The activity introduces students to simple tissue cells and examinations using a microscope.

12* *Columbus Day* (officially observed on the second Monday of October). On this day, we take time to honor and remember Christopher Columbus who sailed across the Atlantic Ocean and made landfall on the island of Hispaniola. He set sail on August 3, 1492. His three ships were the *Niña*, the *Pinta*, and the *Santa Maria*.

Why was Columbus so successful in navigating his three ships? As early as the twelfth century, navigators relied on the compass to help them chart their courses.

Activity Sheet 2.5 allows students to make their own compasses and learn more about magnets. A compass helps people find directions on Earth's surface. It contains a needle that acts as a natural magnet. The needle is attracted to Earth's magnetic field.

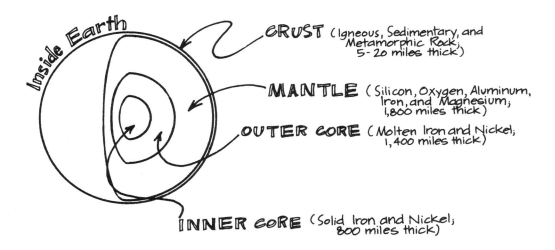

Inside Earth

CRUST (Igneous, Sedimentary, and Metamorphic Rock; 5-20 miles thick)

MANTLE (Silicon, Oxygen, Aluminum, Iron, and Magnesium; 1,800 miles thick)

OUTER CORE (Molten Iron and Nickel; 1,400 miles thick)

INNER CORE (Solid Iron and Nickel; 800 miles thick)

Earth's core contains iron and nickel. Earth is a giant magnet with a north-south field. Children can have fun learning about compasses and the principles of magnetism on Columbus Day using Activity Sheet 2.5 as their learning tool.

15* *National Poetry Day.* This is a time to write a poem about nature, science, or the fall season. It's an opportunity to combine language arts with science. Have the students use Activity Sheet 2.6 to create their own poems on this special day.

One of the most famous poets of all time, the Roman poet Virgil, was born on this day in 70 B.C. He wrote many works, including ten pastoral poems known as the *Eclogues* and twelve complete books of the *Aeneid,* an epic that he was still writing at the time of his death in 19 B.C.

17* *Birthday of Mae C. Jemison, first African American woman in space (born 1956).* Jemison, currently director of the Jemison Institute for Advancing Technology in Developing Countries, completed an eight-day mission in space aboard the space shuttle *Endeavor* on September 12, 1992. As a science mission specialist, she conducted space-sickness experiments and research on bone loss in zero gravity. A Web site that your students could visit is www.quest.arc.nasa.gov/women/TODTWD/ jemison.bio.html.

Have students work in groups to do research on Jemison, the NASA shuttle *Endeavor,* and zero gravity using a KWL chart (KWL is shorthand for "what I *know,* and what I *want* to learn, and what I *learned*"; see Activity Sheet 2.7). Here students pose questions about what they want to learn and write about what they found out.

Find Where the Wind Goes is a publication you may want to share with your students. See Appendix 2 for ordering information.

21* *Birthday of Jay N. Darling, founder of the National Wildlife Federation (1876).* Jay "Ding" Darling was born in Norwood, Michigan. He is particularly famous for his political cartoons, for which he won the Pulitzer Prize in 1924 and 1943.

As head of the U.S. Biological Survey, Darling was instrumental in having land set aside for wildlife refuge and helping fund projects for wildlife conservation. He became president of the National Wildlife Federation and received the Audubon Medal for his outstanding contributions.

Since October is a peak time for the migration of certain birds and butterflies, this is the time to observe and learn more about animal and insect migration patterns. (See Activity Sheet 2.8.)

You will certainly want your students to read some publications by the National Wildlife Federation and the National Audubon Society. For information, visit the National Audubon Society's Web site at www.audubon.org/ and the National Wildlife Federation's Web site at www.nwf.org.

22* *Birthday of Stephen Moulton Babcock, father of scientific dairying (1843).* Babcock was an American agricultural research chemist who developed the Babcock test, a processing technique that measures the quantity of butterfat in milk. This discovery, in which the fat was separated from the milk, led to a great improvement in milk and cheese production. Babcock's research in both the chemistry of vitamins and in nutrition and dairying was significant. He died in 1931.

Have students complete Activity Sheet 2.9 where they will compare the nutrition labels from two cartons of milk. You may also want to talk to them about the different types of milk that they drink and about choosing milk with less butterfat. You could also visit a dairy farm or have a guest speaker from a local university that has a school of agriculture talk to your students about the dairying process.

Web sites you may want to visit include the National Dairy Council at www.nationaldairycouncil.org and the University of Guelph's site on dairy products at www.foodsci.uoguelph.ca/dairyedu/home.html. Here you will find out more about clarification used to purify milk and how the fat globules are separated by the means of a centrifuge, the process that Babcock created.

You may also want the students to examine their milk at home and bring in a nutrition label to compare. They could compare buttermilk, whole milk, skim milk, 2 percent, and 1 percent milk for different nutritional facts. Also, some containers of milk have light blocks, a special bottle that protects milk from light, known to break down vitamins A, C, and B_2. Some milk is fortified with extra vitamin C so that instead of the normal 4 percent, it has 25 percent of the daily value.

24* *Birthday of Anton van Leeuwenhoek, Dutch microscopist (1632).* Introduce your students to (or review) the parts of a microscope, and use a microscope for observations. You may want to order prepared slides from a biological supply house, order live protozoan cultures, examine some pond water (if available), or make an infusion from hay and water. (Appendix 2 gives ordering information for cultures and slides.)

Van Leeuwenhoek studied different forms of plant and animal life and wrote about the life cycles of the flea, ant, and fish. He ground microscope

lenses and even built microscopes himself to study cells, which is known as the science of cytology.

Van Leeuwenhoek was a keen observer and was well known for his work with protozoa and their life cycles. There are excellent science videos and DVDs available that will help your students understand the dynamics of life in a drop of water, as displayed by an amoeba in Activity Sheet 2.10. See Appendix 3 for video and DVD correlations. Visit these online resources for an amoeba printout and for a digital video of an amoeba: www.enchantedlearning.com/subjects/protists/amoeba.shtml and www.micro.magnet.fsu.edu/moviegallery/pondscum/protozoa/amoeba.

Last Sunday in October* *Daylight saving time ends.* On the last Sunday in October, standard time goes into effect. "Spring ahead, fall back" reminds us to set our clocks back one hour.

Time of day depends on the rotation of Earth, which has twenty-four time zones. The width of each zone is 15 degrees longitude. Going east from your time zone, standard time in the adjacent zone is one hour later than in your time zone. Going west from your zone, standard time in the adjacent zone is one hour earlier than in your zone.

The four standard time zones in the continental United States are Pacific, Mountain, Central, and Eastern. Standard time is also known as *Greenwich mean time.* Greenwich is a section of London where time is officially measured. Degrees of longitude and the time zones are calculated to the east and west of Greenwich. Daylight saving time was originated to conserve fuel during times of war and crisis. There is also a Uniform Time Act, legislation that minimizes the variations in time. Most states change their clocks from daylight saving time to standard time and vice versa, but there are some areas that do not.

Acquaint your students with the map provided on Activity Sheet 2.11, as well as a globe showing the lines of longitudes (distance in degrees and minutes from the prime meridian, the imaginary line extending from the North Pole to the South Pole and passing through Greenwich, England—zero degrees longitude).

28 *Birthday of Bill Gates (1955).* Bill Gates, chairman and chief software architect of Microsoft Corporation, was an early computer genius: at age thirteen, he began programming computers. As an undergraduate at Harvard, he continued his programming passion and created a version of Basic, a computer language for the first microcomputer. Have your students visit Gates's own biographical Web site to learn more about his achievements and philanthropy, including the Bill & Melinda Gates Foundation: www.microsoft.com/billgates/bio.asp.

Activity Sheet 2.1.

National Child Health Day

Good food choices, meaning eating healthy food, will lead you and others on the right path of good nutrition.

Help this Olympic runner get fit by making the correct food choices. Follow the healthy food path and win the gold at the end of the maze. If you select the healthy foods in the paths, you'll help this Olympic runner be number 1.

Extra credit: Make up your own food maze to show wise and healthy food choices.

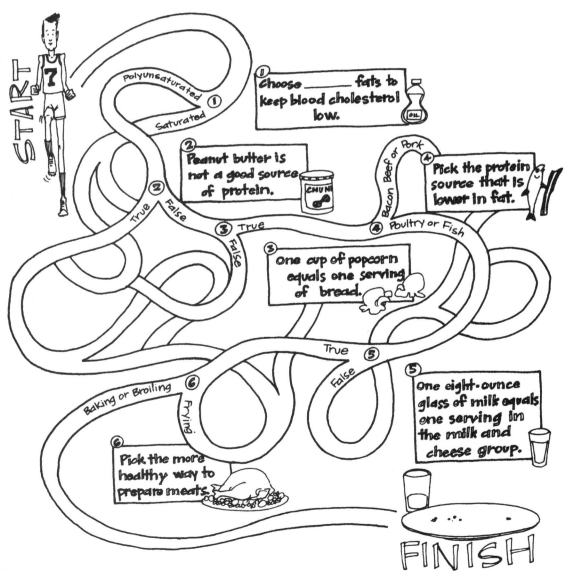

National Child Health Day *(Cont'd.)*

Visit this Web site for information on the vocabulary words: http://www.foodfit.com/healthy/nutritiondictionary.asp.

> **Vocabulary**
>
> protein
>
> cholesterol
>
> saturated fats
>
> polyunsaturated fats

What did you eat today? List them here. Would the foods be considered healthy and nutritious?

_____

_____

_____

_____

_____

_____

_____

_____

_____

_____

_____

_____

Activity Sheet 2.2.

What Does Fire Need to Burn?

The second week in October is Fire Prevention Week. Understanding how to control and use fire is important. Fire can be a useful and helpful tool for cooking, heating, and lighting.

Fire Prevention Week is a good time to learn about fire and fire prevention. You may want to interview some firefighters from your local fire station. This is also a good time to find out about the latest advances in firefighting equipment, from fire extinguishers to fire trucks.

In this investigation, you will find out one way to extinguish fire.

> **Warning:** Adult supervision required.

Materials

clay

5 birthday candles of the same size

nonflammable surface (tabletop)

4 glass jars of different heights

matches

Procedure

1. Make five clay balls to support the five birthday candles. Put the clay and the candles on the nonflammable surface.

2. Line up the jars from smallest to tallest. After lighting the candles, invert the jars and put them over four of the candles. One candle will remain uncovered.

3. Observe the length of time the candles remain lit. Record which is the first to go out, the second, and so forth.

Conclusions

1. Which candle stayed lit the longest? Why?

2. What does fire need to burn?

Activity Sheet 2.3.

Basic Food Groups

During National School Lunch Week, you may want to plan a menu for your school for one day or a whole week. In order to do so, you need to know about the basic food groups. One activity you can do is to invite guests to a well-balanced nutritional meal planned by your class, reflecting the food groups. An invitation is provided that you can use.

The chart provides information about the food groups and the number of suggested daily servings. Read about the types of food in each group, as well as their important contributions.

Food Group	Suggested Daily Servings	Contribution	Examples
Bread, Cereal, Rice and Pasta	6–11	Fiber, Vitamin B, Iron, Protein, Carbohydrates	Cereal, Bread, Pasta
Vegetables	3–5	Fiber, Vitamins, Minerals, Carbohydrates	Potatoes, Beets, Leafy vegetables
Fruits	2–4	Vitamins, Fibers, Minerals	Apples, Oranges
Milk, Yogurt, & Cheese	2–3	Vitamins, Fat, Protein, Calcium	Cheese, Yogurt, Eggs, Cream, Milk
Meat, Poultry, Fish, Dry Beans, Eggs, & Nuts	2–3	Vitamins, Minerals, Fat, Protein	Fish, Chicken, Eggs, Peanuts, Beef, Seeds, and Beans
Fats, Oils, & Sweets	Use sparingly	Fats provide energy	Vegetable/plant oils, Cookies

Basic Food Groups *(Cont'd.)*

Now complete the "My Eating Habits" chart. Enter the foods that you eat in a given day for each meal and any snacks. Sort them by categories and when you eat them. Then think about your eating habits. What conclusions can you make about the types of foods you eat? Do you make nutritious choices? Could you make any healthy improvements?

Invite parents and special guests to your school for lunch after decorating the invitation. Decide with your teacher and school dietitian which day and meal would be best for you to plan. Then send out your invitations and enjoy your special day.

You may want to make the recipe for pumpkin bread. There is also a health and nutrition crossword puzzle for you to solve in this activity.

For details on the food pyramid or to print your own food poster, go to kidshealth.org/kid/stay_healthy/food/pyramid.html and www.mypyramid.gov. You can play the My Pyramid Blastoff game at http://mypyramid.gov/kids/kids_game.html#

Vocabulary	
carbohydrates	amino acids

Date: _____

MY EATING HABITS
LIST OF WHAT I ATE TODAY

MEAL	BREADS & CEREAL	MILK PRODUCTS	FRUITS & VEGGIES	MEAT, FISH, POULTRY, BEANS	TIME
Breakfast					
Lunch					
Dinner					
Snacks					

What FATS did you eat today? _____

You are cordially invited

to come to _____
(name of school)

on _____
(date)

at _____
(time)

for a special luncheon planned by

_____
(class)

We have been studying about proper nutrition,
and we have planned the menu for lunch.

Won't you join us?

Sincerely,

_____

R.S.V.P.

Yes _____
No _____   Signed _____
(guest's name)

P.S.   The cost of the luncheon is _____ per person.
(amount)

56

Basic Food Groups *(Cont'd.)*

Here is a date you won't want to forget: October 31! Halloween has been celebrated for many centuries, but not always with the fashion and flair it is today. It was originally a religious observance, with people attempting to get rid of evil spirits prior to All Saints Day on November 1. Fire festivals were held to frighten away ghosts and witches and black cats—any kind of perceived demons that people feared.

As the centuries passed, customs changed. In the United States, costumes became popular in the late nineteenth century, as did the "tricks." The "treats" came later. The carved jack-o'-lantern contains a lighted candle to scare away any evil spirits and to guard the house it decorates. People in some other countries have carved other vegetables, such as the turnip, to use as their lanterns.

Pumpkin Bread

3 cups flour	4 eggs
3 cups sugar	2 cups pumpkin
2 tsp. baking soda	1 cup vegetable oil
1 tsp. cinnamon	¾ cup water
1 tsp. nutmeg	1 tsp. salt

1. Sift the flour and all dry ingredients. Place in a large mixing bowl.

2. In a separate bowl, beat the eggs. Add the pumpkin, oil, and water. Mix together well. Pour this mixture into the center of the dry ingredients and mix well with a mixing spoon. Do not overbeat.

3. Pour the mixture into two greased and very lightly floured 9-by-5-inch bread pans. Bake for 1 hour at 350°F. Cool in the pan for 10 minutes. Remove from the pan to cool before cutting.

HEALTH & NUTRITION CROSSWORD PUZZLE

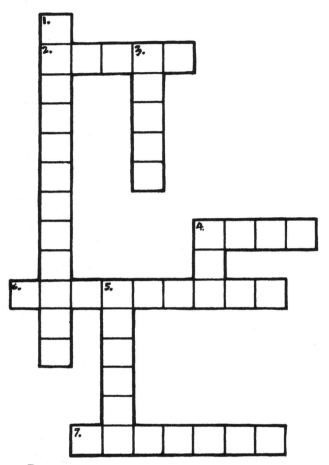

Across

2. I belong to the fruit group. I am a good source of vitamin A and am used in juices, pie, and cider.

4. I belong to the meat group, but am found in the sea. I am lower in fat than red meat and am a good source of protein.

6. I belong to the meat group and am popular in the United States. I have just as much protein as a piece of steak my size, and, if you select me extra lean, I have less fat.

7. I combine amino acids and elements like oxygen, nitrogen, carbon, iron, and hydrogen to help your cells grow well. I also help your hair shine.

Down

1. I am found in breads, fruits, and vegetables. I help give you energy.

3. I am rich in iron and belong to the meat group.

4. I am a fruit. I grow on a tree. I am a source of protein, iron, and vitamin A. I rhyme with *pig*.

5. I am higher in cholesterol than my substitute, margarine. I am a dairy product.

Activity Sheet 2.4.

Examining Tissue Cells

In this activity, you will get to examine your own mouth cheek cells with a microscope.

Materials

depressed glass slide

microscope

medicine dropper

iodine solution (**Caution:** Teacher assistance required)

flat toothpick

Procedure

1. Put the slide on the stage of the microscope.

2. Have your teacher use the medicine dropper to dispense one drop of iodine solution into the well of the depressed slide.

3. Take the flat (unpointed) end of the toothpick and gently scrape the inside lining of your mouth cheek. Put this tissue into the depressed slide with the iodine mixture.

4. Focus the microscope to observe the cells. Adjust both fine and coarse measurements slowly, lowering the microscope to obtain a clear focus. Adjust the mirror and light of the microscope for best viewing.

5. In the space below, illustrate what you see.

Examining Tissue Cells *(Cont'd.)*

Conclusions

1. Make an illustration of one of your slides, and visit this Web site to compare your sketch with your cheek cells: www.botit.botany.wisc.edu/ images/130/Plant_Cell/Animal_cells/cheek_cells.html.

2. What does each cell of tissue contain?

3. How are these cells similar to other cells in your body? Think about their structure.

Want to Learn More?

Read about the scientist Louis-Antoine Ranvier, a French physician who researched human cells.

Activity Sheet 2.5.

Understanding the Compass

A compass helps you locate directions on Earth's surface. It contains a needle that acts as a natural magnet. The compass contains magnetite, also called lodestone. The needle is attracted to Earth's magnetic field.

Let's make a compass to locate Earth's magnetic field. The Earth's core contains iron and nickel. Earth is a giant magnet with a north-south field. Other magnets take on the same orientation. A compass is a good indicator of the north and south poles of Earth's magnetic field, which are different from the geographic North and South Poles, the extreme ends of Earth's axis. In fact, Earth's magnetic South Pole is near the geographic North Pole.

Materials

straight pin

bar magnet

cork disk

dish ¾ filled with water

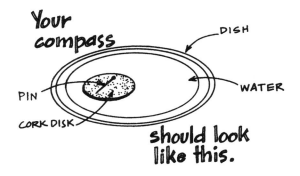

Your compass should look like this.

DISH

WATER

PIN

CORK DISK

Understanding the Compass *(Cont'd.)*

Procedure

1. Stroke the pin in one direction on the bar magnet. Do this about 20 times, using only one end of the magnet and always stroking in the same direction. You have just made a temporary magnet.

2. Float the cork in the water. Place the pin on top of the cork.

3. Watch the movement of the cork and the pin. This is your compass.

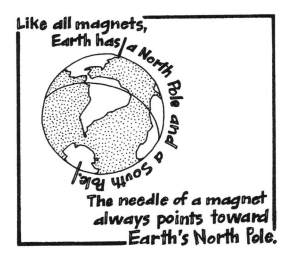

Like all magnets, Earth has a North Pole and a South Pole.

The needle of a magnet always points toward Earth's North Pole.

Conclusion

1. Which way does the pin point, and why?

2. Can you summarize how the magnetic field of the compass interacts with Earth's magnetic field? Describe the movements of your compass.

62

Activity Sheet 2.6.

National Poetry Day is October 15. In the scroll here, write a science poem to celebrate.

Name _____   Date _____

Space and Weightlessness

A KWL chart helps you see what you *know*, what you *want* to learn, and what you have *learned*. Conduct research with a team or by yourself to complete the KWL chart below on the topic of weightlessness and space. You may want to visit the Web site of Mae C. Jemison, the first African American woman in space. Jemison was a science mission specialist aboard the shuttle *Endeavor* and spent eight days in space doing research about space sickness and bone loss in weightlessness. Learn more about Mae Jemison at www.quest.arc.nasa. gov/women/TODTWD/jemison.bio.html. You may also want to visit your library to find biographies on her. To learn more about weightlessness, visit www.spaceadventures.com/steps/zerog.

In the first column, record what you know about weightlessness. In the second column, write some words or phrases to help your research. In the third column, write about what you discovered.

My KWL Chart Weightlessness and Space		
1 What I Know	2 What I Want to Learn	3 What I Learned from My Research

Activity Sheet 2.8.

Why Migration?

Many animals and insects relocate or move their homes seasonally or annually for special reasons. Several of these migrators are listed below, but their names are scrambled. First, unscramble the names; then match the name of the animal or insect with its picture.

Select three migrators and find out about their unique migration pattern. Where does each one go? When? Why? Write that information on the Migration Chart.

Two Web sites you should visit are www.learner.org/jnorth and encarta.msn.com/encyclopedia_761557464/Animal_Migration.html.

Vocabulary
migration

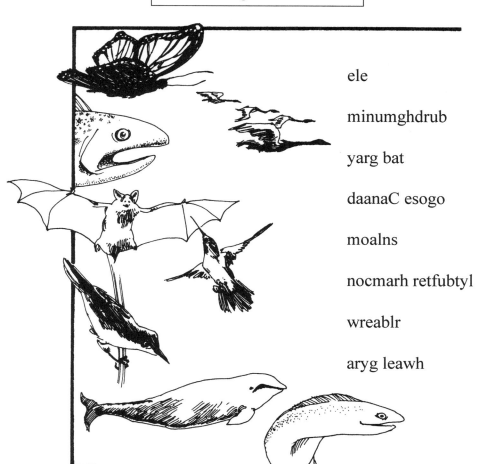

ele

minumghdrub

yarg bat

daanaC esogo

moalns

nocmarh retfubtyl

wreablr

aryg leawh

Name _____   Date _____

Migration Chart

NAME OF ANIMAL	DESTINATION	WHEN?	WHY?
Example: Monarch butterfly	Mexico from Canada	Fall	to lay eggs en route

Now, you write about three other migrators below.

1.

_____

2.

_____

3.

Activity Sheet 2.9.

Milk and Its Nutritional Content

When you buy milk at the store, read the label on the carton. Not all types of milk contain the same healthy ingredients.

Go with your parent to a store that sells milk. Look at the labels listing the ingredients of two different kinds of milk, such as fat-free milk and whole milk. Compare and contrast them. Which would be better for your health, and why? Read the labels carefully, and write your responses to the questions below. For more information or updates on food labels, visit www.fda.gov/label.html.

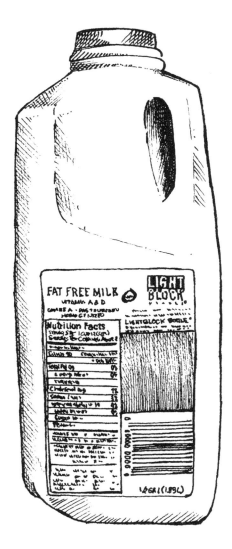

Milk and Its Nutritional
Content *(Cont'd.)*

Which carton has more total fat? _____

Which carton has more saturated fat? _____

Which carton has more cholesterol? _____

Which carton has more sugar? _____

Which carton has more protein? _____

Which carton has more sodium? _____

Which carton has more calories? _____

Which carton has more vitamin D? _____

Which carton has more vitamin C? _____

Which carton has more calcium? _____

Which carton has more vitamin A? _____

Some milk cartons are designed with a "light block" feature to keep the milk fresher for a longer time. Why do you think this helps preserve the milk?

Activity Sheet 2.10.

The Microscope and the Amoeba

In 1665, Robert Hooke made one of the first reports of microscopic study of cells by examining thin slices of cork and naming the little sections or spaces in the cork *cellulae* (cells). About the same time, Anton van Leeuwenhoek built microscopes and used them to examine human blood cells. Both scientists contributed to our understanding and use of the microscope. Do you know how microscopes used today differ from the earlier ones used by Hooke and van Leeuwenhoek? Do a little research to find out.

Here is a chance for you to learn more about single-celled animals like the amoeba. This one-celled animal has parts of its anatomy similar to those found in other protozoa. Examine live or slide-preserved amoeba specimens through a microscope. Look at the words in the Word Box. Then read the sentences and write the correct words in the spaces:

1. I am the "brain" or command center of this cell. I am the _____.

2. I "outline" or define the shape of the cell. I appear in different forms as the amoeba moves, but I am always there. I also control who or what enters or penetrates my wall. I am the _____.

3. I am the center of the cell that processes the food for the amoeba. I help in digestion. I am the _____.

4. If the amoeba needs to eliminate wastes or water, it needs me. I am the

_____.

Visit these Web online resources: www.enchantedlearning.com/subjects/ protists/amoeba.shtm/ for an amoeba printout and micro.magnet.fsu.edu/movie gallery/pondscum/protozoa/amoeba for a digital video gallery of the amoeba.

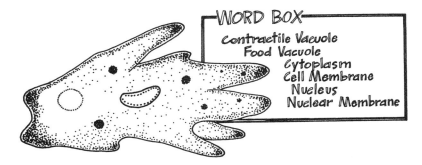

WORD BOX
Contractile Vacuole
Food Vacuole
Cytoplasm
Cell Membrane
Nucleus
Nuclear Membrane

Activity Sheet 2.11.

Standard Time

This map shows the four standard time zones in the continental United States. The meridian for each time zone is listed below. Read the zones, meridians, and times of day. Then fill in the hands on the four matching clocks. Use this information to compute the clock time problems on the next page.

Time Zone	Time Meridian	Clock	Time of Day
Eastern	75°W		5:00
Central	90°W		4:00
Mountain	105°W		3:00
Pacific	120°W		2:00

Standard Time *(Cont'd.)*

Vocabulary
meridian

Look at the clocks below. Each has a special standard time zone and a defined time. Write in the missing time for each clock.

Pacific: 2:00

Central: _____

Eastern: 5:00

Mountain: _____

Mountain: 9:00

Central: _____

Into how many standard time zones of 15 degrees longitude is Earth divided? _____

How many hours difference is there between each zone? _____

How many time zones are there in the continental United States? _____

Can a city have more than one time zone? _____

Visit these three online resources:

www.worldtimezone.com

www.standardtime.com

www.time.gov/timezone.cgi/Eastern/d/-S/java

OCTOBER

1

2 Let's use a microscope today and examine your tissue cells. Use Sheet 2.4.

3

4 In 1959, some of the first photographs of the moon were taken by the Soviet spacecraft *Luna 3.* Find an interesting photograph of the moon. Write a few moon facts on your Mini-Report Form.

5 Do you know who was the first woman to walk in space? Play the October trivia game to learn more. Mix the cards with your September trivia cards for more fun.

6 The first Monday in October is National Child Health Day. Improve your food smarts by making healthy food choices in the fun maze on Activity Sheet 2.1.

ORBIT OF SPUTNIK 1

PHOTO ALBUM OF THE MOON

OCTOBER

7

8 The second week in October is Fire Prevention Week. What does fire need to burn? Let's investigate this question by using Activity Sheet 2.2.

9 FUN FACT: The rose is the national flower of the United States.

10

11

12 Columbus made landfall in North America on this date in 1492. Let's make a special compass using Activity Sheet 2.5.

OCTOBER

13 School Lunch Week follows the second Sunday in October.

14 Plan a school meal.

15 Today is National Poetry Day. Use Activity Sheet 2.6 to write a science poem.

What is the object pictured to the right? Play October Trivia to find out more.

16 In 1846 on this day, an anesthetic was first used in surgery. Invite a dentist to visit your classroom and talk about ways to keep your teeth and gums healthy.

17 Happy Birthday to Dr. Mae Jemison. Learn more about Dr. Jemison and her space research using Activity Sheet 2.7.

18

OCTOBER

19

20

21 Who invented the first electric light?
October Trivia has the answer.
Find out about migration using Activity Sheet
2.8. Jay N. Darling, founder of the National
Wildlife Federation, was born today.
Visit www.nwf.org.

22 Who is the father of scientific dairying?
Learn more about milk nutrition with
Activity Sheet 2.9.

23

24 Let's use a microscope today to find out more about
tiny one-celled animals. Use Activity Sheet 2.10.

OCTOBER

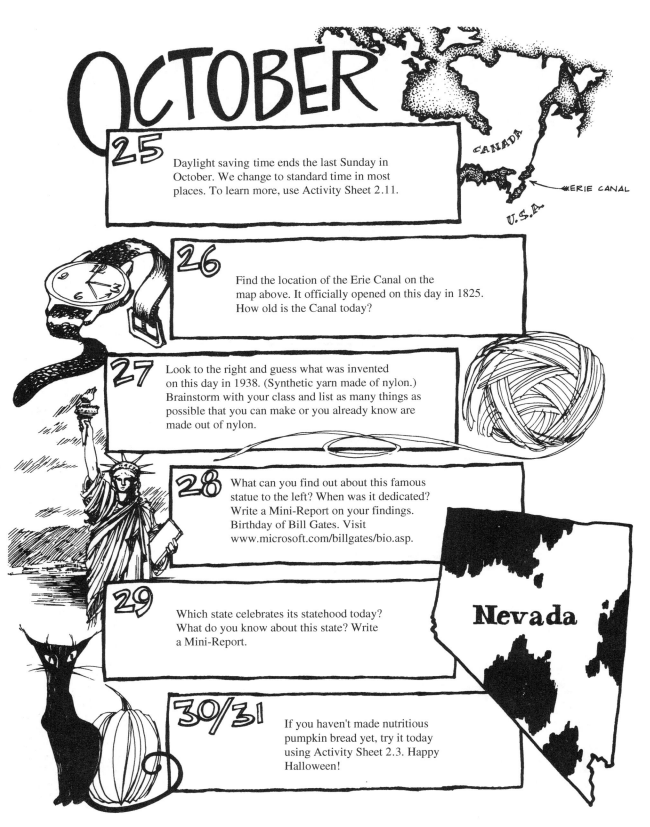

25 Daylight saving time ends the last Sunday in October. We change to standard time in most places. To learn more, use Activity Sheet 2.11.

26 Find the location of the Erie Canal on the map above. It officially opened on this day in 1825. How old is the Canal today?

27 Look to the right and guess what was invented on this day in 1938. (Synthetic yarn made of nylon.) Brainstorm with your class and list as many things as possible that you can make or you already know are made out of nylon.

28 What can you find out about this famous statue to the left? When was it dedicated? Write a Mini-Report on your findings. Birthday of Bill Gates. Visit www.microsoft.com/billgates/bio.asp.

29 Which state celebrates its statehood today? What do you know about this state? Write a Mini-Report.

30/31 If you haven't made nutritious pumpkin bread yet, try it today using Activity Sheet 2.3. Happy Halloween!

November

November is a good month to do a unit on space and the solar system. There are notable events that can be related to one another and to some developments in space exploration. Feel free to use the activity sheets at any time during the school year, either singly or as a set.

You will probably want to work with your school or public librarian to bring together as many books and visual resources as possible for your students on the following topics: space explorers and astronauts, the solar system, nutrition and fitness for space explorers, and examination of spacecraft.

Write to the National Aeronautics and Space Administration (NASA) for free classroom materials. Many of the activities correlated with the entries for November here are reprinted with permission of NASA or have been adapted from its *Student Liftoff Resource Kit*. You will also want to review the list of correlated videos and DVDs in Appendix 3.

The information provided for each entry is background information for you. Feel free to consult other sources for further details, including NASA and the correlated videos. Also consult your school science materials and texts.

Some November Dates to Remember and Background Information for the Activities

Activity sheets are provided for starred dates only. It is your decision whether to give the students facts on each entry. And for the trivia game referred to, go to Appendix 5.

1* *U.S. Weather Bureau's first meteorological forecasts were recorded based on the use of a telegraph (1870).* Activity Sheet 3.1 will give your students some information on cloud types, as well as firsthand experience in observing weather and correlating precipitation with types of clouds.

3* *First dog in space on* Sputnik 2 *(1957).* Before people went into space, other animals began their missions. There were nine *Sputnik*s launched by the Soviet Union, beginning with *Sputnik 1* on October 4, 1957. The Space Age was officially launched.

The capsule of *Sputnik 1* weighed 184 pounds. This spacecraft remained in orbit until it burned up in the atmosphere in 1958.

Sputnik 2 carried a small dog named Laika. Although the dog did not survive the mission, Laika's contributions prepared the way for human space travel in the future.

Activity Sheet 3.2 is adapted with permission from NASA. It was developed by Science Weekly, Inc., for its Operation Liftoff Space Science Program in 1987. The activity sheet will help your students understand that proper nutrition and eating are essential to survival and travel in space. The food and its preparation are the focus of this activity. Students will learn how foods can be rehydrated in space.

4 *Discovery of King Tutankhamen's tomb in Egypt (1922).* Although no activity sheet is provided for this entry, it is worth mentioning the discovery of this tomb on this date and including a brief summary of its chronology, especially for more advanced students.

The young King Tutankhamen (King Tut) ruled Egypt from 1361 B.C. to 1352 B.C., yet it was not until A.D. 1922 that the English Egyptologist Howard Carter discovered his burial tomb and its chambers in Luxor, Egypt, on the West Bank of the Valley of the Kings. The gold mask and many other treasures have become symbols of the young king's dynasty. Your students may want to read about archaeologists and some of their methods of excavation.

7 *Birth date of two physicists, Marie Curie (1867) and Lise Meitner (1878).* Although no activity sheets are provided for these two scientists, you may want to use the Famous Person Chart (in Activity Sheet 4.1) or Nobel Prize Award Form (in Activity Sheet 4.3) in Chapter Four. Both sheets encourage students to read and find out about outstanding scientists.

Marie Curie won the Nobel Prize twice, in 1903 for physics and in 1911 for chemistry. She is famous for the discovery of the radioactive elements polonium and radium and her research on radioactivity. She was the first woman professor to teach at the Sorbonne in Paris.

Lise Meitner's research led to the discovery of uranium fission. She was a German physicist who received recognition for her science research.

Depending on the grade level and abilities of your students, this date could initiate a class research project on the contributions of women as pioneers in science. This would be more appropriate for upper-intermediate students, focusing also on careers in science.

9* *Birthday of Carl Sagan (1934).* This U.S. astronomer, biologist, author, and television personality died on December 20, 1996. His research and involvement in the U.S. space program, including the expeditions of the *Mariner, Viking,* and *Voyager* spacecrafts, helped us understand the atmospheric conditions and composition of many planets, including Saturn and its largest moon, Titan. Have students research the Web or go to the library for books and articles about Titan and Saturn, and then complete Activity 3.3, a crossword puzzle about Titan.

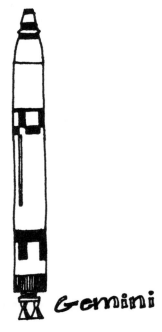

Titan, in Greek mythology, refers to the family of "giants." Indeed, Saturn's moon, Titan, is the second largest satellite in the solar system. The diameter of Titan is 3,200 miles (5,150 kilometers) and its surface temperature is –290°F (–179°C). On January 14, 2005, the Cassini spacecraft with the Huygens probe (Christian Huygens discovered Saturn in 1655) penetrated the red haze of its atmosphere to take photos, analyze chemicals, measure wind, and record sounds on Titan. The atmosphere is 95 percent nitrogen and 3 percent methane. The atmosphere is 1.6 times that of Earth, and half the satellite is made up of water in the form of ice and half of solid rock.

Visit www.nineplanets.org to find out more about the moons in our solar system.

11* *U.S. space milestone—Gemini 12 launched (1966).* Activity Sheet 3.4 is provided to mark this milestone in space exploration. The *Gemini* missions were the second phase of the U.S. space program and were aimed at reaching the moon. Project *Mercury*, a single-person spacecraft, was the first part. The *Gemini* carried two crew members and was followed by the *Apollo* flights—all the more challenging because they involved launching a three-member crew into space.

Each launching and space milestone resulted in the achievement of certain goals. In these early missions, the goal was to reach the moon, which was accomplished with the *Apollo 11* landing on July 20, 1969.

This is a good opportunity to learn about and compare the differences in spacecraft. The *Gemini* had 50 cubic feet of space for its crew and measured 11 feet long and 7½ feet across its base. It was more complex than the *Mercury*, but not as complex as the *Apollo* spacecraft, which boasted 210 cubic feet for its crew and had three parts to it.

The *Gemini* was designed to provide experience in docking and rendezvous techniques, critical to a safe return to Earth. There were ten manned flights of the *Gemini* from March 1965 until November 1966.

14* Apollo 12 *lands on the moon (1969).* The first moon landing was completed by Neil Armstrong and Edwin Aldrin Jr. (with Michael Collins in orbit) on July 20, 1969. The successful voyage of *Apollo 11* changed the direction of lunar science. The landing was watched live on television by more than 500 million people.

NASA's mission report describes the application of the *Apollo 11* knowledge in the *Apollo 12* landing and mission as "a thousand, maybe even a million times more important to science . . . while the rocks brought back by *Apollo 11* were a geologic hors d'oeuvre, the samples collected by *Apollo 12* were a veritable feast."*

The lunar rock samples help answer questions about the origin of the moon, its geological features, and the universe in general. The astronauts brought back approximately seventy-five pounds of moon rock. Some of the rocks contained crystals longer than one inch, indicating that the moon once consisted of hot, igneous rocks. Perhaps the moon was hot as long as 1 billion years ago. Volcanic activity may have caused the melting of the rocks.

The lunar samples contained no hydrated minerals, implying that water did not exist when they were formed. While *Apollo 11* samples had more breccia, a rock like clay or sand with sharp embedded fragments, that constituted only 5 percent of the *Apollo 12* sample.

---

*NASA, *Apollo 12 Mission Report*, p. 2.

There are two activity sheets for this entry to help your students understand astronauts' lunar discoveries. From their observations and lunar walks and from studies of the samples they returned to Earth, our knowledge of the moon has increased in depth and breadth.

Activity Sheet 3.5 introduces students to types of lunar rocks.

Igneous—rocks that are formed when molten rock (magma) cools and solidifies

Spinel—attractive gemstone minerals that are commonly red

Feldspar—a group of rock-forming minerals that makes up as much as 60 percent of the world's crust

Anorthosite—an igneous rock, mostly consisting of feldspar

Breccia—a rock like clay or sand with sharp embedded fragments

Activity Sheet 3.6 helps students understand how astronauts work in a weightless environment, as when they are orbiting in a spacecraft. Activity Sheet 3.6 is adapted from the *Student Liftoff Resource Kit,* provided and distributed by NASA. (See Appendix 3 for video and DVD correlations.)

You will certainly want to combine these activity sheets with information on the moon. Have your students read about the moon and write to NASA for publications and free classroom materials.

Scientists have learned much about the moon from studying the sample rocks returned by the astronauts on missions like *Apollo 11* and *Apollo 12.* They believe that the moon's upper crust (thirty to sixty miles thick) is different from its interior. The fact that it has an upper crust means that its early geological history was similar to Earth's, although the moon's crust is much thicker than that of Earth.

Scientists also found out that the moon is very quiet in terms of seismic events. "Moonquakes" do occur, but only a few hundred happen during a year in relation to more than a million quakes on Earth. Visit these space, star, and moon Web sites:

http://www.earthsky.org/shows/astrophysics.php

www.teachervision.fen.com/page/1530.html

http://solarsystem.jpl.nasa.gov/planets/profile.cfm?Object=Moon

Study of the lunar rocks also gives information about the magnetic field of the moon—a much smaller magnetic field unit than Earth's. The moon's measurement was 35 gamma, whereas Earth's is about 50,000 gamma. (Gamma is a unit of measurement of light and magnetism.) The natural magnetism found in the lunar rocks probably accounts for the low and steady magnetic reading that the astronauts measured.

Finally, the large amount of natural glass found in the moon rock samples reveals that meteoroid impacts caused the abundance of this glass, which they found in the specimens brought back to Earth. Glass in the lunar rocks has survived more than 4 billion years, whereas our glass on Earth is only 200 million years old. The process of devitrification, where glass changes into its component minerals, is much slower on the moon because of the lack of water there.

Share some of this knowledge of Earth and the moon gained from study of the lunar rocks brought back by the *Apollo* missions.

17* *Birthday of John Stanley Plaskett (1865).* Plaskett was a Canadian astronomer famous for his observations and design of a space spectrograph, an instrument used to observe stars. A space spectrograph allows a probe to go deeper into the universe using special features, filters, and detectors. Have students complete Activity Sheet 3.7 to understand the differences in star types and magnitude and brightness of stars. Generally the hotter the star, the brighter the star. Help students compare the sun, which is a G-type star (5,500°C or 10,000°F), to an O star, which can be seven times hotter (40,000°C or 72,000°F). Star types, from hottest to coolest, are O, B, A, F, G, K, and M, which students are often taught to remember as "Oh, Be A Fine Girl (or Guy)—Kiss Me!" Our galaxy, the Milky Way, has 200 billion stars.

The seven brightest stars in our galaxy, in order of brightness, are Sirius, Canopus, Alpha Centauri, Arcturus, Vega, Capella, and Rigel.

Students will visit several Web sites for information on star brightness.

25* *First artificial heart transplant (1984).* In 1984, Dr. William De Vries performed a successful artificial heart transplant. Developing and surgically implanting the artificial heart required knowledge of the human heart, the nervous system, and the circulatory system. Activity Sheet 3.8 helps students identify the parts of the heart and become aware of their pulse and heartbeat and the changes in pulse rate before and after exercise.

Exercise and nutrition are important to maintaining a healthy heart. Regular exercise is an encouraged part of anyone's lifestyle, even astronauts in space.

Astronauts who did not exercise while in space suffered muscular and bone deterioration, especially in environments without gravity. Treadmills are now provided on space shuttles, and astronauts exercise for at least fifteen to thirty minutes daily. Their blood pressure is regularly monitored too.

Taking care of your heart through proper diet and exercise can prolong the health of your heart and prevent damage and deterioration.

27* *Birthday of Anders Celsius (1701).* Anders Celsius was born in Uppsala, Sweden. He was a professor of astronomy and is credited with inventing the Celsius thermometer. He was also interested in the aurora borealis (northern lights), which he observed more than three hundred times.

The Celsius temperature scale is also called the centigrade temperature scale. It is based on 0° as the freezing point of water and 100° as the boiling point of water. Celsius invented the scale in 1742.

Have your students use the following formula (or demonstrate for them) to convert a temperature from its equivalent Fahrenheit reading to Celsius:

$$\text{degrees Celsius} = 5/9 \times (\text{degrees Fahrenheit} - 32)$$

Activity Sheet 3.9 will give students practice with these conversions, along with some practical applications to better understand daily body temperatures.

Activity Sheet 3.10 will familiarize your students with cosmic radiation, a source of energy found in space that consists of heated particles that move with higher speeds. In 1984, tomato seeds were sent into space and exposed to cosmic radiation for six years, returned and then shared with students in 1990. More than 12.5 million seeds traveled in space. When the seeds were returned, they were distributed to schools across the country. The space seeds grew into plants that at first appeared greener in color, since they had more chlorophyll and carotenes than regular Earth seeds and plants. However, over time, they did not produce better or larger plants.

Encourage students to think scientifically about experimenting with plants. Discuss plant research going on today or conduct an experiment in your own classroom. You could grow plants from the same batch of seed and expose some seeds to stronger light and other seeds to no light. Try a combination of various factors, but be sure to keep certain variables the same, like the amount of water used for each seed. Have your students monitor the experiment and discuss the results.

Activity Sheet 3.1.

Investigating Cloud Types

Do you regularly observe the shape, color, and type of clouds above you? Each day, clouds provide information about the weather and changes we might expect to occur.

Vocabulary		
condensation	cumulus	stratus

Clouds have different shapes, colors, thicknesses, and names. They are formed from water vapor in Earth's atmosphere. The condensation forms from the water vapor being cooled.

Most clouds are either cumulus- or stratus-type clouds. *Cumulus* are puffy clouds, appearing at different heights. *Stratus* are layered clouds.

For the next four days, observe the clouds in your area, and record your information in the observation chart here. Consult a book on clouds; then identify the type of cloud, the weather at the time of recording, and the time. Finally, write a paragraph or two to summarize your observations and findings about cloud types.

What predictions can you make regarding the weather from the information you found?

Visit these Web sites:

www.uen.org/utahlink/weather/
　　clouds/cloud_id.html

www.metoffice.com/bookshelf/
　　clouds/

www.geo.mtu.edu/department/
　　classes/ge406/jmparke/

Investigating Cloud Types *(Cont'd.)*

	Time	am. or p.m.	Cloud Type	Weather Conditions
Day One 1.				
2.				
3.				
Day Two 1.				
2.				
3.				
Day Three 1.				
2.				
3.				
Day Four 1.				
2.				
3.				

Activity Sheet 3.2.

Nutrition in Space

This activity will help you understand the role of good nutrition and healthy eating for space travelers. Since proper eating is essential to survival, the foods selected and taken on the space voyage must be carefully chosen. They must be easy to prepare, be lightweight, and need no refrigeration. They must also be compact since storage space is minimal on board a spacecraft.

What is a "dehydrated" food? Write the definition at the bottom of this sheet or on your science vocabulary form. Do you know where the astronaut gets water on board the spacecraft to rehydrate the food? From the shuttle's fuel cells. They combine oxygen and hydrogen to make electricity and produce water in the process.

A typical dehydrated dinner for an astronaut might be shrimp cocktail, rice, steak, vegetable, pudding, and grape drink.

Can you imagine standing on your head and chewing? Astronauts must eat and chew very carefully and slowly. To learn more about space food, visit these two Web sites: www.liftoff.msfc.nasa.gov/academy/astronauts/food.html and www.liftoff.msfc.nasa.gov/academy/astronauts/food-history.html.

Nutrition in Space *(Cont'd.)*

Look at the Word Box below. Match the words on the left to their definitions on the right. Then write a paragraph listing what you would eat for three balanced meals for one day in space. (Foods like eggs, cereals, and strawberries can be dehydrated.)

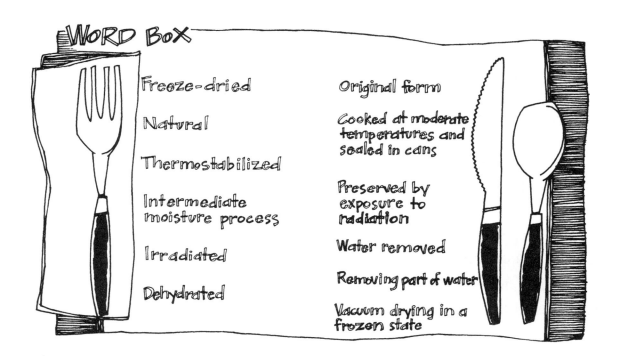

WORD BOX

Freeze-dried

Natural

Thermostabilized

Intermediate moisture process

Irradiated

Dehydrated

Original form

Cooked at moderate temperatures and sealed in cans

Preserved by exposure to radiation

Water removed

Removing part of water

Vacuum drying in a frozen state

Nutrition in Space *(Cont'd.)*

Rehydration Investigation

Do this rehydration investigation to find out how much rehydrated foods weigh. What does "rehydrated" mean?

Warning: Adult supervision is required for this investigation.

Materials

scale

bowl

single-serving package of dehydrated soup mix

spoon

250 ml boiling water

Procedure

1. Weigh the empty bowl, and record its weight here: _____

2. Weigh the soup mix before rehydrating, and record its weight here:

   _____

3. Empty the package of soup mix into the bowl. Have an adult pour the boiling water into the bowl. Stir.

4. Weigh the rehydrated soup and record here: _____

Conclusion

1. What is the difference in weight between the dehydrated soup and the rehydrated soup?

2. Why are dehydrated foods taken on space missions?

Activity Sheet 3.3.

Exploring Saturn's Largest Moon

Saturn is the second largest planet in our solar system. Seven rings, made mostly of ice, surround it. Research Saturn and list some important facts, including the name of the largest of Saturn's moons. To learn more, visit www.kidsastronomy.com/saturn/moons.htm or www.enchantedlearning.com/subjects/astronomy/planets/saturn/saturnmoons.shtm/.

Be a space sleuth and see if you can discover the answers to this fun crossword puzzle either online or in a book about Saturn's moons.

Across

1. Saturn's largest moon

3. An atmospheric gas found there

7. In Greek mythology, the name for superbig or Titan meant this

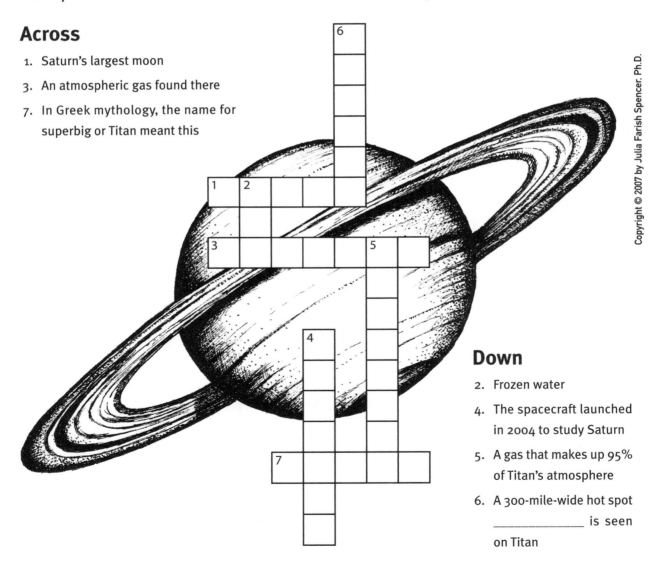

Down

2. Frozen water

4. The spacecraft launched in 2004 to study Saturn

5. A gas that makes up 95% of Titan's atmosphere

6. A 300-mile-wide hot spot _____ is seen on Titan

Name _____   Date _____

Investigating Spacecraft

There were three early space programs aimed at putting a person on the Moon: Projects *Mercury, Gemini,* and *Apollo.*

Here is a chance for you to examine the differences among the spacecraft used in these three projects. Look at the illustrations and statistical information about each spacecraft on the next page. For further background information, you will want to visit Web sites and learn the comparative differences among these spacecraft.

What differences do you notice in their size (height and weight)? What do you notice about the seating capacity? How about the volume inside the spacecraft? Read about each one, and complete the chart below. Visit these two Web sites for additional information: www.apollo-society.org/merc_gem_apollo.html and www.thespaceplace.com/history/mercury/mercury06.html.

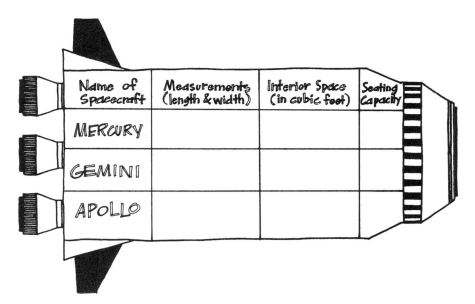

Name of Spacecraft	Measurements (length & width)	Interior Space (in cubic feet)	Seating Capacity
MERCURY			
GEMINI			
APOLLO			

Conclusion

How much more space (cubic feet) did *Apollo* have in its crew compartment than *Mercury*? Than *Gemini*? How do you think this extra space might benefit the crew? Can you explain this? Visit the suggested Web sites above, and compare and contrast the three spacecrafts and their successes.

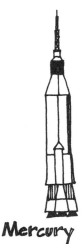

Mercury

Six manned launches from May 1961 to May 1963

STATISTICS: 36 cubic feet in crew compartment; 9.5 feet long, 6 feet across base

SEATING CAPACITY: 1

Eleven manned launches from October 1968 to December 1972

STATISTICS: 210 cubic feet in crew compartment; 157 cubic feet in lunar module

SEATING CAPACITY: 3

Ten manned launches from March 1965 to November 1966

STATISTICS: 50 cubic feet in crew compartment

SEATING CAPACITY: 2

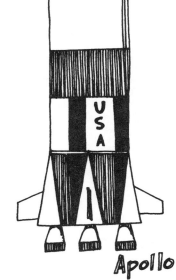

Gemini

Apollo

92

Name _____   Date _____

Activity Sheet 3.5.

Be a Lunar Rockhound

See if you can match the type of rock with the definition or information provided. These rocks were discovered by our astronauts in their early missions to the moon. From examining the rock samples, scientists have found out much about the history of the rocks, the universe, and the moon. Although many of the rocks were billions of years old, they were in excellent condition, free of signs of weathering.

WORD BOX

Igneous   **Feldspar**   **Breccia**

Spinel   **Anorthosite**

1. I am a rock found on the Moon. I contain bits of broken rocks, minerals, and glass. When a "meteorite" hit the surface of the Moon, I was

   formed. I am a _____.

2. I represent the type of rock formed by volcanic activity. I started as a liquid and became solid rock containing minerals and crystals. I am

   _____ rock.

3. I am a mineral found in different rocks. I look beautiful and flawless like a gem. I come in many colors, or I can be clear, like a diamond. I am

   _____.

4. I am a mineral that is often found in granite. I have a pinkish hue or color. I'm used in common household cleaners. I'm frequently found in

   lunar rocks. My name is _____.

5. I'm a special rock because I contain mostly one mineral, feldspar, with a little olivine mixed in. It took people a little longer to find me . . . I was

   hiding in the Moon's highlands. Who am I? _____

Activity Sheet 3.6.

A Weightless Environment

Copyright © 2007 by Julia Farish Spencer, Ph.D.

When we work and play on Earth, we are influenced by the pull of gravity. Gravity actually helps make our jobs easier to perform. It weighs us down so that we do not float around, as we and all other objects would. That is not the case in a spacecraft, where there is almost no gravity. Astronauts have found that working in a weightless environment requires more energy. Can you imagine floating around in space without being attached to anything?

Astronauts working in their spacecraft found that moving around was more difficult than on Earth. Bending down to pick up items wasn't as easy as they thought. Straightening themselves back up in a cumbersome space suit added to their difficulty. Astronauts continue to learn with each mission, resulting in improvements and changes in space suits and equipment.

What happens to objects in a "weightless" environment? Does water drip down or float up? Could this be dangerous? What does this mean in terms of planning and preparation prior to flight? See if you can find out more about how astronauts drink and wash in space. Write to NASA if you like. Scientists use the term *microgravity* to describe the small amount of weight people and objects actually have in space. This may be a new word to define for your Vocabulary List.

Also visit the NASA Web site at www.nasa.gov/home.

Draw a drop of water coming from this faucet as if it were in a weightless environment.

A Weightless Environment *(Cont'd.)*

Think about the pull of gravity in the following investigation.

Materials

plastic milk container (rinsed and dried)

scissors

wide rubber band

hook on a wall

30 marbles

Procedure

1. Hang the plastic milk container by cutting and tying one end of the rubber band to the handle and the other end to a hook on the wall.
2. Fill the container with 10 of the marbles.
3. Watch and observe the rubber band. What happens?
4. Repeat steps 2 and 3, adding another 10 marbles. Then add the final 10 marbles and watch what happens.

Conclusions

1. What happens to the rubber band? Why?
2. How does this show the pull of gravity?
3. How do you think weightlessness changes your body? Your height? Your appearance? Did you know weightlessness can make your shoes get loose and your waist smaller?

Special thanks to NASA and
"Living in Space" for this investigation.

Activity Sheet 3.7.

Star Match

Stars are made up of gases like helium and hydrogen. We can observe stars from Earth because they emit light and are bright. Visit these Web sites to learn more about stars and their brightness: www.space.about.com/od/basics/a/starmagnitudes.htm, www.astro.wisc.edu/~dolan/constellations/extra/brightest.html, and www.infoplease.com/pa/A0004435.html.

The brighter the star, the hotter the star! The lower the magnitude, the brighter the star!

Be a star and try to match correctly all the star names to the constellations. A star's magnitude or brightness is measured from 1 to 6. A 6 rating means that you can see the dimmest star with the naked eye. A 1 rating means it is 100 times as bright as a star rated 6.

All of these stars listed below are less than 1 on the brightness scale, which makes them the seven brightest stars in our galaxy of 200 billion stars.

Put a numeral in front of each star name so that numeral 1 represents the brightest star in this group. Then draw a line from the name of the star to its correct constellation.

The first one is done for you.

Copyright © 2007 by Julia Farish Spencer, Ph.D.

1	Sirius (−1.46) Blue-white star	Lyra (The Harp)
___	Alpha Centauri (−.27) Yellow-white star	Canis Major (The Big Dog)
___	Vega (.03) Blue-white	Centaurus (Centaur)
___	Canopus (−.72) White	Orion (The Hunter)
___	Arcturus (−.04) Orange	Carina (The Keel)
___	Capella (.08) Yellow-white	Auriga (The Charioteer)
___	Rigel (.12) Blue	Böotes (The Herdsman)

96

Activity Sheet 3.8.

Aerobics in Space?

Whether living in space or on Earth, taking good care of your heart is essential. Regular exercise and good nutrition are important to a healthy heart. Find out how astronauts exercise in space. How does it compare with how you exercise on Earth?

Look at the illustration of the heart below. Select words from the Word Box, and fill them in on the correct lines. Then complete the exercise on measuring your pulse.

left ventricle	right atrium
superior vena cava	pulmonary artery
cardiac veins and arteries	left atrium
right ventricle	pulmonary veins
aorta	

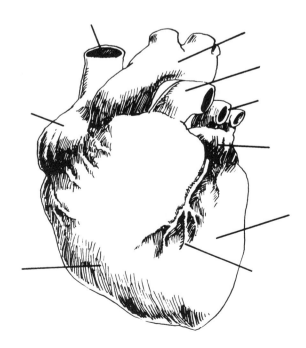

Aerobics in Space? *(Cont'd.)*

Materials

stethoscope

clock or watch with a sweep second hand

Procedure

1. Use the stethoscope to listen to someone else's heart. This is the normal sound of the heart at rest.

2. Use your index and middle fingers to find that person's pulse beat from his or her wrist. Count the number of beats that you feel for 15 seconds.

   Record that number here: _____.

   Multiply it by 4 and record it here: _____. That is the pulse rate for 1 minute at rest.

3. Now ask the person to run in place for 1 minute. Repeat step 2. Listen to the person's heart with the stethoscope.

4. Record all the information in the chart below.

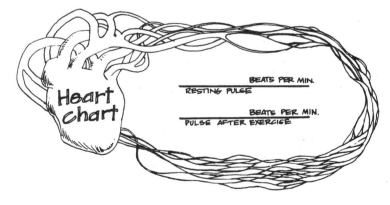

Heart chart

RESTING PULSE _____ BEATS PER MIN.

PULSE AFTER EXERCISE _____ BEATS PER MIN.

Conclusion

1. What is a pulse rate? Define it.

2. How did the exercise change the pulse rate?

Activity Sheet 3.9.

Celsius Degrees

The Celsius temperature scale was invented by Anders Celsius in 1742. It is a standardized scale in which the interval between the freezing point of water and the boiling point of water is divided into 100 degrees.

In the Celsius scale, water freezes at 0° and boils at 100°.

To change a reading in Fahrenheit to Celsius, use this formula:

$$°C = 5/9 \times (°F - 32)$$

NASA has reported that the spacesuit the Apollo astronauts wore protected them from extreme temperatures ranging from −250°F to 250°F.

Using the formula invented by Celsius, convert those two temperature readings from the Fahrenheit scale to the Celsius scale. Show your computations on the back of this sheet, and write your answers below.

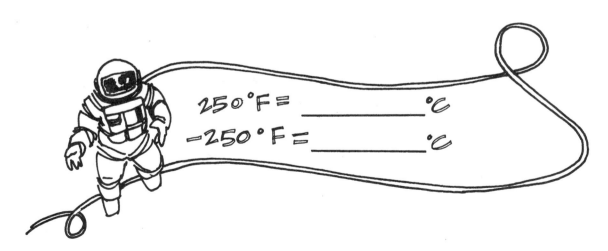

250°F = _____ °C

−250°F = _____ °C

Celsius Degrees *(Cont'd.)*

Now convert the following body temperatures:

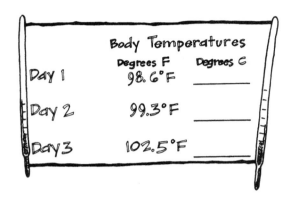

Body Temperatures

	Degrees F	Degrees C
Day 1	98.6°F	_____
Day 2	99.3°F	_____
Day 3	102.5°F	_____

> Normal, healthy body temperature ranges from 97° to 100°F. Body temperature fluctuates during the day depending on activity, general health, and food and water intake. A temperature above 100° is considered a fever.

These are three Web sites you might find helpful for understanding body and Celsius temperatures:

www.my.webmd.com/hw/health_guide_atoz/hw198785.asp

www.energyquest.ca.gov/scientists/celsius.html

www.wbuf.noaa.gov/tempfc.htm

Activity Sheet 3.10.

Tomatoes from Space

In March 1990, tomato seeds that were orbiting Earth in a spacecraft originally launched in 1984 were returned to Earth and distributed to schools. These special seeds had been exposed to cosmic radiation for six years in space. *Cosmic radiation* is a source of energy found in space that consists of heated particles that move with higher speeds. Children and teachers nationwide participated in growing and harvesting these tomato plants. At first, the space seeds grew into plants that appeared greener in color, since they had more chlorophyll and carotenes than regular Earth seeds and plants. However, over time they did not produce better or larger plants. To learn more about cosmic radiation, visit http://helios.gsfc.nasa.gov/cosmic.html.

Research has shown that radiation to plants can result in the introduction and creation of genetic mutations and variations in offspring plants. Genetic mutations are changes to the genetic material (the stuff that all living things are made of) in a cell. The pink grapefruit is the result, for example, of an experiment with radiating the white grapefruit.

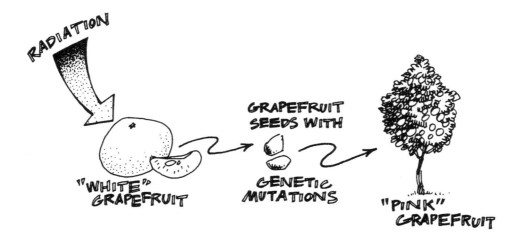

101

Tomatoes from Space *(Cont'd.)*

What do you think the future holds? What other types of seeds might be exposed to cosmic radiation and brought back to Earth? Why do you think NASA selected tomato seeds for this experiment?

Brainstorm these questions with your classmates and teacher. Talk about your predictions for the future. Then fill in a few observations and thoughts about space food on the tomatoes sheet on the next page. A helpful science dictionary can be found at www.enchantedlearning.com/science/dictionary.

Tomatoes from Space *(Cont'd.)*

NOVEMBER

1 Praise the U.S. Weather Bureau as it celebrates its first forecast using a telegraph (1870). Make your own forecasts after observing cloud types, using Activity Sheet 3.1.

2

3 What are dehydrated foods? How are they rehydrated in space? Have fun with Activity Sheet 3.2 to learn more.

Play November Trivia to learn the name of the first dog in space.

4 Who was King Tut? Who found his tomb in Egypt in 1922? What was found in the tomb? Play November Trivia.

5

6

NOVEMBER

7 Who was Marie Curie? Who was Lise Meitner? Why are they remembered today?

Play November Trivia to learn more.

8

9 Happy Birthday to Carl Sagan. This former U.S. astronomer researched Saturn and its moon, Titan. Complete a space crossword puzzle using Activity Sheet 3.3.

10

11 Learn more about spacecraft using Activity Sheet 3.4.

12

NOVEMBER

13

14 What was *Apollo 12* and where did it land
on this day in 1969? Play November Trivia to find
out. Activity Sheets 3.5 and 3.6 will help you
learn more about rock collecting on the moon.

15

16

17 Star Match: Have fun using Activity Sheet 3.7.
Learn about the stars and their brightness!

18

NOVEMBER

19

20

21

22

23

24

NOVEMBER

25

Play November Trivia to learn about an important surgical procedure performed on this day in 1984. Use Activity Sheet 3.8 to learn about space aerobics and how to keep your heart fit.

26

27

Let's play with temperature scales, using Activity Sheet 3.9. Happy birthday to Anders Celsius. Who was he? Visit www.energyquest.ca.gov/scientists/celsius.html.

28

29

30

December

December is organized to celebrate and recognize many famous people. It is also a festive month with the celebration of Hanukkah, Christmas, Kwanzaa, and other festivals worldwide.

December is the month that recognizes the official arrival of winter with the winter solstice. It is a time to appreciate and recognize nature and the environment by caring for certain animals, plants, and flowers—including the holiday favorites of mistletoe, poinsettia, and evergreen trees.

The activities presented this month highlight the gifts or contributions of people in our past and the study of nature and the environment. This underlying theme will give unity to your presentations and activities.

Some December Dates to Remember and Background Information for the Activities

Activity sheets are provided for starred dates only. It is your decision whether to give the students facts on each entry. And for the trivia game referred to, go to Appendix 5.

1* *First day of the month.* Have your students make a special calendar that focuses on the contributions of famous people born or recognized this month. Look over this list of entries. Then select those that you want to highlight this month for your students according to their age, interests, and abilities.

One idea is to have a large master calendar (or bulletin board) and enter symbols or pictures of these famous people on the appropriate date block. This will allow you to use the calendar repeatedly for months other than December. For example, for December 8, you may want to glue some cotton on the calendar in honor of Eli Whitney. For December 9, you could paste a picture from a box of frozen foods in honor of Clarence Birdseye, the naturalist who developed the process of freezing foods. And on December 16, you may want to honor Margaret Mead.

You may also want to display the students' "Famous Person Chart" (see Activity Sheet 4.1) recognizing famous people. You could also trim a real or artificial tree and decorate it with symbols and pictures of these famous people and their inventions and discoveries.

3 *The first human heart transplant (1967).* On December 3, 1967, a team of thirty people, headed by Doctor Christiaan N. Barnard, performed the first human heart transplant. The recipient, Louis Washkansky, age fifty-five, lived until December 21, 1967. Although he did not live long following his surgery, the operation medically influenced future heart transplants. If you decide to share this information with your students, relate the important contribution and bravery of people such as Louis Washkansky who gave their lives for medical advances such as this. Their contributions to others are immeasurable.

8* *Birthday of Eli Whitney, inventor of the cotton gin (1765).* On March 14, 1794, Eli Whitney received an official patent for the cotton gin, a machine used to tear the cotton fiber from the seed. There was considerable dispute and litigation over his invention. The net result was that Whitney himself realized little monetary profit from it, but the South prospered by the use of this invention, both in time saved and financial prosperity. Whitney's patent expired in 1807, and it was not renewed by Congress.

Whitney went on to apply many of the principles he learned in college and in his experience with the cotton gin to create a system of mass production, supplying parts of muskets to the government for their military supplies (1801). You might have students complete the "Famous Person Chart" (Activity Sheet 4.1) for this entry. You may also want to use September's "Patent an Invention" (Activity Sheet 1.3) if you did not use it in September.

9* *Birthday of Clarence Birdseye (1886).* Birdseye, a naturalist, inventor, and businessman, developed his process for freezing foods from his observations of freezing methods used in Labrador, where he spent time as a fur trader. Often people's inventions or discoveries stem from their early experiences, jobs, or observations.

Birdseye used two metal plates that could be refrigerated to freeze foods effectively. His preservation techniques were so successful in retaining flavor and taste that his products were quickly accepted. His company, General Seafoods, was bought by another company and renamed General Foods Corporation.

This is a good time to talk to your students about freezing foods as a process of preservation. Help students find out about proper freezing techniques (how to wrap and store food; how long to freeze food; what temperatures are recommended) as well as the recommended storage times for different foods. Then have students complete Activity Sheet 4.2.

10* *Nobel Prize: A Who's Who.* On this day in Stockholm and in Oslo, the Nobel Prize is awarded to laureates in six areas: physics, physiology or medicine, chemistry, peace, literature, and economic science.

The first award was made in 1902, on the fifth anniversary of the death of Alfred Bernhard Nobel, a Swedish chemist. Nobel invented dynamite, as well as other explosives, and left a sizable fortune in trust, which goes toward the prize each year. Up to three individuals in each area may share a Nobel Prize. The laureates receive a gold medal and a diploma in addition to money.

Activity Sheet 4.3 will help your students research this year's Nobel Prize winners in science. The crossword puzzle will help them learn about some of the past laureates.

ALFRED B. NOBEL

11* *Birthday of Annie Jump Cannon (1863).* An astronomer who specialized in stellar spectra, Cannon was an assistant at Harvard College Observatory from 1897 to 1911. She also discovered several stars and novae.

Activity Sheet 4.4 will give your students a chance to identify five different constellations. It will also encourage them to read and find out about stars and novae.

You may want to combine this activity with mention of Johannes Kepler, father of modern astronomy, recognized this month on December 26. If career exploration in science is appropriate, have students find out about careers in astronomy.

12* *Birthday of Alfred Werner (1866).* Alfred Werner, a winner of the Nobel Prize in Chemistry in 1913, is remembered today. Either Activity Sheet 4.1 or Activity Sheet 4.3 may be used. Werner studied the structure of chemical compounds and bonding. His research contributed to understanding the basis of inorganic chemistry. (This entry may be more appropriate for more advanced students.)

15* *Birthday of Charles Augustus Young (1934).* Activity Sheet 4.1 can be used to research the career and contributions of Charles Augustus Young, an American astronomer who studied the sun and concluded that Earth's magnetic conditions are affected by the sun's solar disturbances. Famous for his solar photography, Young contributed to our understanding of the sun's corona and its eclipses. Since this month recognizes the winter solstice (occurring between December 20 and 23), talk to the students about that day having the shortest amount of sunlight in the Northern Hemisphere in the year.

16* *Birthday of Margaret Mead, American anthropologist (1901).* Activity Sheet 4.1 may be used for biographical research. Mead, who received her doctorate from Columbia University in 1929, was a keen observer of cultures and people and wrote twenty-three books. She became a curator of ethnology at the American Museum of Natural History in New York City. Here are two interesting science career options for your students to investigate: anthropologist and curator.

17* *Orville and Wilbur Wright successfully completed the first manned power flight (1903).* This historical record was set in Kitty Hawk, North Carolina. (See the entry for December 26, George Cayley.)

On their fourth attempt Wilbur flew 852 feet in 59 seconds. History was made!

Prior to this historic date, the Wright brothers had built three biplane gliders. They had observed the natural flight patterns of large, soaring birds, including hawks, vultures, and eagles, as well as the wing movement of birds. Their observations led them to develop three-axis control and other principles of control still used today. Share with the students how the Wright brothers' discovery was based on observation of animal (bird) locomotion. They took what they saw and applied the principles to machinery.

FLYER III

Flyer III, their third biplane glider, was able to stay in flight for half an hour. It had its own engine and propellers as well. The Wright brothers contributed much to the science of aviation.

Many of the famous inventors and scientists mentioned in December used their gifts of observation and their intuitive minds to create their inventions. Whether it was Birdseye in Labrador, Mead in Samoa, Whitney in Georgia, or the Wright brothers in North Carolina, they all were keen observers and thought scientifically about what they saw.

The first jet engine was invented in 1930 by British pilot Frank Whittle. Jet engines used gas propulsion rather than propellers to move aircraft. Activity Sheet 4.5 allows students to observe the propulsion of a balloon as the gases escape from the inflated balloon through an extended straw.

19* *Distribution of the first issue of* Poor Richard's Almanack *(1732).* "Poor Richard" was the pen name of Benjamin Franklin, one of America's most famous scientists, statesmen, and inventors. The character created in this early almanac was a quiet countryman who dispensed wisdom and information to his readers. Among the more famous of his quotations is "Early to bed and early to rise makes a man healthy, wealthy, and wise."

Activity Sheet 4.6 contains an almanac evaluation chart. Students can select, review, and compare different almanacs and write a report or evaluation on one or more of them. You may want your more advanced students to write entries for their own almanac, using the blank dates on the December calendar sheets. Students could do Activity Sheet 4.1 on Benjamin Franklin.

December 19 also recognizes the first radio broadcast from space in 1958, from the U.S. satellite *Atlas,* a message from President Dwight D. Eisenhower: "To all mankind, America's wish for peace on Earth and good will toward men everywhere." The entire message was fifty-eight words. Two almanac Web sites to visit are www.infoplease.com/almanacs.html and www.factmonster.com/almanacs.html.

20–23 *The winter solstice announces the official arrival of winter.* This is the shortest day of the year and the first day of winter for the Northern Hemisphere and the first day of summer for the Southern Hemisphere. Have your students use the Science Current Events form in Appendix 6 to write about the solstice. Newspapers often feature information on the solstice, as do other books. Johannes Kepler (see December 26) discovered that Earth revolves around the sun in an elliptical path. You have the option of presenting this information today.

25 *Christmas.* (Do this activity prior to vacation.) In December we recognize many religious days, including Christmas, Hanukkah, and other holidays that you may want to discuss with your students prior to their vacation. You may want to relate these days to the festive ways trees, flowers, and plants are used and decorated during these times of celebration. Students can write a report using the mini-report form in Appendix 6, or they can create holiday trivia game cards using the templates in Appendix 5.

25* *Birthday of Clara Barton (1821).* Activity Sheet 4.1 can be used to remember Clara Barton, the founder of the American Red Cross. Many students may not know about this organization and how it operates. You may want to contact the Red Cross for information for your school or arrange to have a guest speaker visit the school. Visit www.redcross.org for information.

Barton was a former school teacher and later a clerk in the U.S. Patent Office. During several wars, she organized and obtained relief in terms of food, medicine, and supplies for soldiers, and she helped victims of other disasters, including earthquakes, cyclones, and floods. She was nicknamed the "angel of the battlefield."

26* *Birth date of Louis Pasteur, French chemist and microbiologist (1822); Johannes Kepler, German astronomer (1571); and George Cayley, English scientist (1773).* All three scientists may be researched with Activity Sheet 4.1. You will probably want to do this and the following activities prior to vacation.

Pasteur studied microorganisms and fermentation and is credited with the development of pasteurization (a process of heating foods and beverages to destroy harmful bacteria). Milk, for example, is pasteurized by heating for half an hour at a temperature of 145°F, followed by cooling. You may want to talk to your class about this process and compare to unpasteurized milk.

Johannes Kepler, the father of modern astronomy, was born in 1571. He discovered that Earth and other planets revolve around the sun in an elliptical pattern. Kepler formulated three laws that describe planetary motion (Kepler's laws). He improved the early telescope for viewing astronomical objects, and his refracting telescope is known as the Keplerian telescope. You may want to share this information with your students on the winter solstice.

George Cayley, the scientist who built and piloted the first manned airplane glider, was born in 1773. He is considered the founder of the science of aerodynamics. Students may be fascinated by finding out about his glider design, complete with tail unit, fuselage, and fixed wings.

You may want to talk with your students and encourage them to think critically about how Cayley's discovery paved the way for the Wright brothers' flight in 1903. Cayley's first flight was in 1853. This gives you the option of using this information on December 17 as well. Two Web sites to visit are www.outerbanks.com/wrightbrothers/wrightlc.htm and www.wright.nasa.gov/wilbur.htm.

28 *Chewing gum patented by William Semple (1869).* Students will have fun discovering the origins of chewing gum. They may have more fun if you honor the day by letting them chew some in class. If the students are having a holiday party prior to vacation, tell them about this date and the patent.

You may want to talk about the different types of gum that are available today. Is chewing gum detrimental to teeth? Are certain types better than others? Are there benefits to chewing gum? You may also use Activity Sheet 1.3 again and have your students create new types of chewing gum for the future.

29* *Charles Macintosh, Scottish chemist, bonded rubber to fabric to create raincoats (1823).* Activity Sheet 4.1 can be used to honor him. After Macintosh patented his fabric in 1823, *mackintosh* became a generic name for waterproof raincoats, particularly in Britain.

31 *First incandescent electric light demonstrated by its inventor, Thomas Edison (1879).* In Menlo Park, New Jersey, Thomas Edison demonstrated the operation of his carbon filament lamp, the first incandescent electric lightbulb able to burn for a reasonable length of time. Edison was a true inventor, creating more than a thousand inventions. For more information, visit www.sln.fi.edu/franklin/inventor/edison.html.

In February, you may want to remember Edison on his birthday or on National Inventor's Day. You have the option of using this activity then or now.

Show your students the parts of an incandescent bulb, and explain what each part is. Then have them complete Activity Sheet 4.7. You may also want to talk to them about the differences between incandescent and fluorescent bulbs. They may be interested to know that Edison began many of his inventions when he was as young as ten years old! As a scientist and inventor, he continued to work throughout his life, creating many worthwhile inventions.

Since so many students see holiday trees and homes decorated with colorful lights at this time of the year, talk about the value, significance, and importance of lights in communicating feelings. Lights are used in cars too, both for safety (to see at night and in foul weather, to signal a turn) and for communicating statements or feelings of support (funerals, campaigns). Students can bring in or talk about different kinds of light-bulbs that are available today (neon, bubble, strobe, plant-grow, colored). Plan a showcase exhibit of different types of lights, perhaps tracing the history of the lightbulb.

Activity Sheet 4.1.

Remembering Special People

Select one or more of the famous people highlighted in your calendar this month. (See the names in the illustration below.) It could be someone who was born in December, someone who demonstrated or patented an invention, or a person who received a special award for his or her discoveries.

Read about that person at your library. The person will be referenced in the encyclopedia and often in other books. Visit the Web for information at www.infoplease.com/almanacs.html and www.factmonster.com/almanacs.html. Take some notes about what the person did, and record facts about his or her life that interest you. Why is the person you selected remembered and honored? Summarize your information on the Famous Person Chart.

Are there people in your school or classroom you might want to honor this month? Brainstorm with your classmates and think about the reasons (special events, birthdays, honors).

FAMOUS PERSON CHART

Name of Famous Person: _____

Place of Birth: _____

Education (List schools attended and degrees obtained):
_____
_____

Career in Science (Tell what the person did):
_____
_____
_____
_____
_____

Major Contribution(s) to Field of Science (Tell what the person is best remembered for—any discoveries or inventions):
_____
_____
_____
_____
_____
_____

Think! Tell why you think this person made a difference. Why was he or she special? Express this in your own words on the other side of this sheet.

This chart was completed by: _____

Name _____   Date _____

Will This Food Last Forever?

Foods can be preserved by wrapping and freezing them at 0°C or below. Moisture- and vaporproof materials are used to wrap the food products, as are special freezing containers. It's a good idea to date and label your frozen foods since their storage time is limited. Try matching the food items in the chart below with the recommended storage time limit in the column to the right. Draw a line to connect the food item with the time limit. For example, commercial ice cream can be stored up to three weeks. Consult a cookbook or search the Web as a reference guide.

On the back of this sheet, write a few statements about how to safely defrost foods.

A useful Web site to visit is www.aces.edu/dept/extcomm/specialty/freezing_foods.html.

FOOD ITEM	RECOMMENDED STORAGE TIME LIMIT
Beef Steaks	8 to 12 months
Fish	2 months
Butter	3 months
Whipped Cream	1 month
Lobster	6 to 9 months
Turkey	6 months
Frosted Cake	3 to 6 months
Doughnuts	2 to 4 weeks

121

Activity Sheet 4.3.

Winners of the Nobel Prize

Look in an encyclopedia or an almanac for a list of all past winners of the Nobel Prize. Also, visit nobelprize.org for a list of all the winners and for more information about the prize. Find out the six different areas or categories in which the prize is awarded, and list them on the back of this sheet. After you've done the research, complete the following Nobel Prize crossword puzzle.

Next, select three people who have received the prize, and enter the information requested on the Nobel Prize Who's Who chart. On the back of that sheet, tell why you think it is important to award this prize.

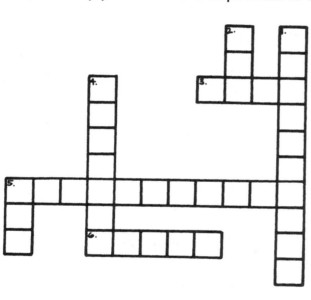

Across

3. The first Nobel Prize (1901) was awarded to Wilhelm Röntgen of Germany for his discovery of radiation composed of these special rays.

5. In 1964, Konrad Bloch (United States) and Feodor Lynen (Germany) received the Nobel Prize in physiology for their discoveries regarding fat consumption and _____ .

6. Last name of the inventor of dynamite.

Winners of the Nobel Prize *(Cont'd.)*

Down

1. A category for the Nobel Prize in biology dealing with living matter.

2. An external organ for hearing.

4. A protein hormone that helps metabolize carbohydrates and is used to control diabetes. (Discovered in 1923.)

5. Name for "feline"; rhymes with "rat."

Nobel Prize Who's Who

MEDAL FOR
PHYSICS
AND CHEMISTRY

MEDAL FOR
ECONOMICS

MEDAL FOR
PHYSIOLOGY OR
MEDICINE

MEDAL FOR
LITERATURE

MEDAL FOR
PEACE

YEAR	RECIPIENT(S)	REASON FOR AWARD	NATION

Activity Sheet 4.4.

Be a Stargazer

There are many books about stars and charts of the stars and the constellations. Go to the library and choose books to read about the stars and constellations. Then write a science mini-report that includes answers to three of the following questions:

1. Which star is the brightest night star? Which is the brightest day star?
2. Did you know that the sun is a star?
3. What are *novae*?
4. What colors are stars?
5. How hot are stars?
6. Do stars move and "rise and set" like the sun does?
7. Can you see the same stars every night of the year? Are the stars you see in summer different from the stars you see in winter?
8. Which is the Dog Star?
9. What is a constellation? Do you know how many constellations are in the sky?

On the next page are five well-known constellations (or parts of them). Look at a star chart and select the correct name from the Word Box. Write the name of each constellation above the constellation.

Here are a couple of useful Web sites to visit for information on stars and constellations: www.kidscosmos.org/kid-stuff/stars-facts.html and www.astro.uiuc.edu/~kaler/sow/sow.html.

Vocabulary
novae

124

Be a Stargazer *(Cont'd.)*

| Lyra | Pegasus | Cygnus | Leo | Orion |

1.

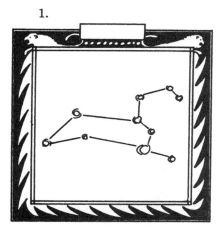

2.

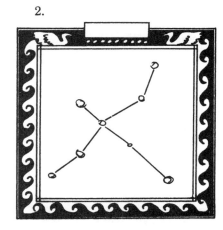

3.

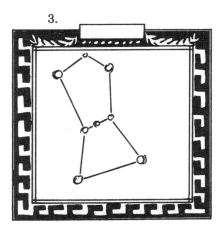

4.

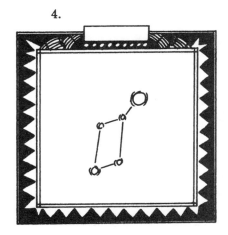

5.

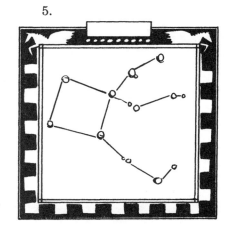

125

Activity Sheet 4.5.

Gases, Propulsion, and the Science of Flight

Vocabulary
propulsion

Materials

plastic straw (cut to fit inside the balloon mouth and extend 1 inch)

balloon

tape or rubber band

sink or a large plastic dishpan

water

Procedure

1. Put the straw into the mouth of the balloon and extend it down 1 inch. Tape or secure it in this position with a rubber band.

2. Fill the pan or sink with water. (Experiment with warm and cold water.)

3. Inflate the balloon, and put your finger over the straw opening until you let the balloon go after placing it on the surface of water. Observe and record your observations. Remember to experiment with warm and cold water.

Make sure you pinch the neck of the balloon after you've blown it up so no air can escape before takeoff!

126

Gases, Propulsion, and the Science of Flight *(Cont'd.)*

Conclusions

1. Tell what happened to the balloon. What made the balloon move?
2. What does this simple investigation tell you about gases and propulsion?
3. How does this relate to airplane propulsion?

For more information, visit these Web sites:

http://wright.nasa.gov/wilbur.htm

www.nasm.si.edu/wrightbrothers

This experiment helps show how the gases in an airplane propel it through the air. But how does an airplane get off the ground? How do airplanes stay aloft for long periods of time without using up huge amounts of fuel? What does a plane have that your balloon does not? Look in the encyclopedia for more information on the science of flight.

Activity Sheet 4.6.

Compare Almanacs

An almanac is a reference work (book or online resource) that lists information about important people, dates, places, and events. There are many types of almanacs published today: children's almanacs, science almanacs, farmers' almanacs, stockbrokers' almanacs, world almanacs, and more! People often give almanacs as holiday gifts.

One of the most famous almanacs was Benjamin Franklin's *Poor Richard's Almanack*, first distributed on December 19, 1732. Ask your school or public librarian to show you a copy of this first almanac.

Then review it and at least one other almanac. Compare the information found in them. What are the similarities? What are the differences? Think about the format, that is, how the material is presented.

Do you like one type of almanac better? Which one? Visit these two Web sites and compare them: www.infoplease.com/almanacs.html and www.factmonster.com/almanacs.html.

Review your favorite almanac, and then fill out My Favorite Almanac Chart.

MY FAVORITE ALMANAC CHART

Title of Almanac: _____

Authors: _____
_____

Publisher: _____

Copyright Date: _____

Table of Contents (List five features of this book you like):

_____
_____
_____
_____
_____
_____
_____

Three Amazing Facts (List three amazing and interesting facts in this book—extra credit for SCIENCE FACTS):

_____
_____
_____
_____
_____
_____
_____
_____
_____
_____
_____
_____

Activity Sheet 4.7.

Remembering Edison

At this time of year, there are many lights burning—tree lights, candlelights, lights in our homes. The incandescent lightbulb was demonstrated for the first time by its inventor, Thomas Alva Edison, on December 31, 1879. Prior to that time, there were no electric lights.

Consider the ways we respect electricity and lights and remember precautions we should take at this busy time of year concerning electric light safety and energy conservation.

Then select the words from the Word Box and match them to this illustration of an incandescent bulb. You may want to visit these two Web sites: www.thomasedison.com and www.sln.fi.edu/franklin/inventor/edison.html.

Word Box

socket	wire
filament	metal strip
gases	insulation

ANOTHER OF EDISON'S INVENTIONS IS THE PHONOGRAPH, OR RECORD PLAYER. INVENTED IN 1877, THE FIRST PHONOGRAPH PLAYED RECORDS THAT WERE CYLINDRICAL (SHAPED LIKE A SODA CAN), NOT FLAT LIKE MODERN ONES. BUT EDISON'S IMAGINATION NEVER STOPPED WORKING. IN THE 1880's HE DEVELOPED THE FIRST TALKING DOLL. THE DOLL HAD A TINY PHONOGRAPHIC CYLINDER IN ITS CHEST THAT COULD BE TURNED WITH A CRANK TO MAKE THE DOLL TALK.

DECEMBER

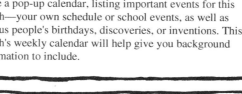

1 Make a pop-up calendar, listing important events for this month—your own schedule or school events, as well as famous people's birthdays, discoveries, or inventions. This month's weekly calendar will help give you background information to include.

2 Or, you may want to make a peek-through-the-doors science calendar and illustrate important people and discoveries for this month. Give your calendar as a holiday gift to be enjoyed year after year.

3 Learn about healthy hearts and how to keep them fit. Have your school nurse or a cardiologist visit your class to discuss this. Six states celebrate their birthdays in December, the month with the most state birthdays. Illinois became the 21st state in 1818.

4

5

6 The first St. Nicholas Day was observed in Turkey over 1,600 years ago!

DECEMBER

7

8 Use the Famous Person Chart on Activity Sheet 4.1 to find out about Eli Whitney, born on this date in 1765.

9 Find out about food storage times using Activity Sheet 4.2. Happy Birthday, Clarence Birdseye. Who was he?

10 The Nobel Prize is awarded today in Oslo and Stockholm. What is the Nobel Prize? Is it given only to scientists? Do a crossword puzzle using Activity Sheet 4.3. Happy Birthday, Mississippi— it became the 20th state in 1817

11 Learn about stars and constellations by using Activity Sheet 4.4. Who was Annie Jump Cannon? Play December Trivia to learn more! Today is Indiana's birthday—it became the 19th state in 1816.

12

DECEMBER

13

14

Alabama became the 22nd state in 1819 today.
Play December Trivia to learn more.

15

American astronomer Charles Augustus Young
was born on this day in 1834. Use Activity Sheet
4.1 to learn more.

16

Anthropologist Margaret Mead was
born on this date in 1901. Play
December Trivia to learn more. Use
Activity Sheet 4.1 if she is your "special person."
The composer Beethoven was born today in 1770.

17

Learn about
gases and the basics
of air propulsion. Use
Activity Sheet 4.5.

18

DECEMBER

19 Learn about the first space broadcast in 1958. Play December Trivia. *Poor Richard's Almanack* was first published on this day in 1732. Use Activity Sheet 4.6.

20 The winter solstice is this week. Look in newspapers for stories or information. Why is this the shortest day of the year? Make your own trivia card and ask a friend to answer it.

21 Winter is here! What is it like in South America? What kind of path does Earth follow in its yearly journey around the sun?

22

23

24

DECEMBER

25 Learn more about the Red Cross. What does it do? How does it help others? The founder of the American Red Cross, Clara Barton, was born on this date in 1821. Use Activity Sheet 4.1 to find out about this "angel of the battlefield."

26 The father of modern astronomy was born today. Play December Trivia to learn more. In southeast Asia, a deadly tsunami occurs. (2004)

27 Use Activity Sheet 4.6 to learn more about tsunamis.

28 Guess what was first patented today in 1869? Look to the right and find the answer. Iowa became the 29th state in 1846. Play December Trivia to learn more.

29 On this date, we celebrate the creation of the first bonded rubber raincoat. Who created it? Play December Trivia. Also, happy birthday to Texas, which became the 28th state in 1845.

30/31 Use Activity Sheet 4.8 to learn more about Thomas Edison and incandescent bulbs. How many different kinds of lightbulbs can you name?

Kipling...Sh

January

This month's chapter introduces students to the forms and composition of matter. To help your students, you should become familiar with the nature of atoms and molecules. This information underlies the scientific principles for many of the activities and investigations this month.

The word *atom* is derived from ancient Greek and means indivisible. Our understanding of the nature of an atom has evolved from the theories of Democritus in the fourth century B.C. and John Dalton in the early nineteenth century. A limited number of basic atoms exist called "elements." All atoms in an element, such as gold, have similar characteristics—size, weight (mass)—and share similar properties.

Atoms combine with other atoms to form molecules. A molecule of water, for example, has two hydrogen atoms and one atom of oxygen, hence H_2O. One drop of water has millions and millions of molecules, so tiny that we can hardly imagine their size. Scientists have gone further in their research on the nature of atoms to conclude that atoms are composed of subatomic particles. Continuing research will add to our understanding of the nature and composition of atoms and molecules.

An atom is composed of particles called neutrons (without a charge), protons (positively charged), and electrons (negatively charged). Electrons orbit (in a dimensional space) around the nucleus of the atom. Electrons can move from one object to another, as in static electricity (see Activity Sheet 5.5), and the electrical charge of the object can therefore change. Normally, an atom has an equal number of protons and electrons, and the atom is electrically neutral, or "uncharged."

If the balance is disturbed or altered, as in static electricity, the atom can become negatively charged if it has more electrons than protons or positively charged if it has more protons than electrons.

As in magnetism, opposites attract. A proton's electrical field attracts negative charges and repels positive charges. An electron follows the same principles: it attracts positive charges and repels negative charges.

An atom may absorb energy, as when something is heated. Atoms and molecules then speed up, often colliding with one another. This can change the state of matter, from solid to liquid or liquid to gas, for example.

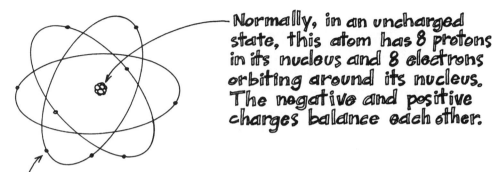

Normally, in an uncharged state, this atom has 8 protons in its nucleus and 8 electrons orbiting around its nucleus. The negative and positive charges balance each other.

If an extra electron "hops" onto this atom, it will now have a negative charge because the negatively charged electrons outnumber the positively charged protons by one.

Some January Dates to Remember and Background Information for the Activities

Activity sheets are provided for starred dates only. It is your decision whether to give the students facts on each entry. And for the trivia game referred to, go to Appendix 5.

1 *Birthday of Paul Revere, American patriot, silversmith, and eyeglass maker (1735).* You may want to mention Paul Revere's birthday and have students research his inventions. They could use the Biographical Sketch form in Appendix 6. You might also have the students compare information they find about Revere and his eyeglasses to the advances in style and eyewear today, and report on their findings.

2 *USSR's* Luna 1 *successfully orbits the sun (1959).* Have the students do a search on the Internet to find out more about the *Luna 1* orbit. You might have them compare orbits and space missions to the various planets, the moon, and the sun, and how the differences in the planets affect the types of space missions that are launched. Also, have them learn more about the sun, which is actually a star. The library and the Internet are excellent resources. One useful Web site for this topic is www.bbc.co.uk/science/space/exploration/missiontimeline/luna1.shtml.

4 *Birthday of Louis Braille (1809).* Braille invented a system of reading and writing for the blind that uses a code of raised dots. The braille system can be used for math and music as well. Ask your students if they've ever seen a book in braille before. Did they touch the pages with their fingertips to see how it feels? Feel free to have students explore books and the Internet to learn more about Louis Braille and the braille system. They will find this Web site useful: www.afb.org/braillebug/louis_braille_bio.asp.

5* *Birthday of early hot-air balloon pilot Jeannette Piccard (1895).* Use Activity Sheet 5.1 to help explain how heat makes gases expand. Have the students complete the activity after visiting this Web site: www. balloonzone.com/history.html. The entry for January 7 has information about successful balloon flight across the English Channel in 1785, almost one hundred years prior to Piccard's adventure. In December, the students studied the history of flight with the Wright brothers. You may want to have them do those activities as well, or if they completed them previously, have them compare how the flights were similar and different. Have them think about how information builds and how scientists learn from one another from both their successes and their failures.

5 *George Washington Carver's birthday (1864).* Have the students use the Who's Who in Science form from Appendix 6 and research Carver and learn about his experimentation and accomplishments with the peanut.

7* *Balloon flight across the English Channel (1785).* This flight was made by Jean-Pierre Blanchard and John Jeffries. When students use Activity Sheet 5.1, they will learn about air temperature and how the molecules in air move at different speeds depending on temperature. When air is warmed, it expands, and the molecules move faster, allowing for greater expansion of the air. Temperature affects matter, especially the molecules in air, which are not fixed, as in a solid.

10 *Birthday of Norman George Heatley (1911).* Norman Heatley is credited with expanding on the findings and discovery of penicillin by Sir Alexander Fleming and making it possible to mass produce penicillin. You may want to talk to the students about the use of modern antibiotics and how they are used to treat infections. Since many school absences occur in January due to infections from colds and flu and secondary infections, this is a good time to discuss Heatley. For more about penicillin, revisit the entry for September 24, and Activity Sheet 1.10, Understanding Mold.

12* *NASA launches Deep Impact spacecraft (2005).* This spacecraft was designed to study comets and the creation of our solar system. For background information, go to www.deepimpact.umd.edu/gallery/bye_bye_ DI.html. The solid nucleus of a comet, which can be miles wide, can be compared to the nucleus of an atom. When the sun melts ice in a comet's nucleus, it creates a cloud of dust, water, vapor, and gas called a *coma.* Have students find out what is in the tail of a comet: ions and dust that have escaped the nucleus of a comet, giving it the long tail effect. The word *comet* comes from the Greek word *kometes,* which means "long-haired." The molecules of water and carbon that appear on Earth may have come from long-ago impacts of comets and their wastes on the planet. More than 65 million years ago, destruction from a major comet may have caused the extinction of dinosaurs on Earth.

Have students complete Activity Sheet 5.2 to learn more about comets. Two useful Web sites about comets are www.windows.ucar.edu/tour/ link=/comets/comets.html and www.nineplanets.org/comets.html.

13* *Stephen Foster Day.* This day recognizes the composer of "Oh! Susanna" and other American folk songs. Use Activity Sheet 5.3 to learn more about how sound travels and how matter changes sound moving through it. Sound is perceived because of the sound waves, which include volume and pitch. Sounds are high and low, and soft and loud. When sound vibrates, the volume depends on the force of the vibrations. Louder sounds make greater vibrations and have more force than softer sounds. Sound energy is produced by the vibrating objects as they travel through matter in sound waves, which can bounce off matter or be absorbed by it. Also, the faster an object vibrates, the greater the sound waves are. When the sound waves are closer together, the faster an object will vibrate. Students will learn more about sound waves in the activity.

Certain forms of matter transmit sound more easily and quickly than others (see Activity Sheet 5.3). Air is a gas, and the molecules have more freedom and space to move. Water is a liquid, and the molecules become denser. Liquids can transmit sound more quickly than gases for that reason. Any state of matter can transmit sound waves. You may want to have your students experiment with molecular movement and sound. If an increase in temperature causes sound waves to travel more quickly, ask the students to think of ways to show this. Would a bell sound different if it were rung indoors or outdoors?

14 *Paleontologists discover dinosaur-eating mammals in Liaoning, China (2005).* What is noteworthy about this event is that science theory changes as new evidence is found. The established theory that mammals never preyed on dinosaurs was reversed when scientists in China found the remains of two interesting mammals that appear to have devoured dinosaurs.

The two dinosaur eaters were *Repenomamus giganticus,* a large doglike mammal, and *R. robustus,* which was about the size of a cat and resembled a Tasmanian devil. Its meal was a parrot dinosaur about five inches in size.

14* *Birthday of David Wesson (1861).* Wesson was an American chemist who invented vegetable oil. He founded the Southern Oil Company after he successfully purified cottonseed oil and perfected a process to make oil more palatable. Students can have fun learning about oil and water with Activity Sheet 5.4. A good Web site to visit is www.library .thinkquest.org/J001539/exp1.html.

By doing the experiment in this activity, students will learn that although both water and oil are liquids, they have different compositions of matter and atoms of molecules. When the liquids separate, students can observe the globules of oil floating in water. This is called an *emulsion.* Detergent is added to the mixture so that the oil molecules change again: they become smaller and better able to dissolve in water.

17* *Birthday of Benjamin Franklin (1706).* See Activity Sheet 5.5. This activity explores the complexity of static electricity. Static electricity runs through a circuit, as does current electricity. In static electricity, the particles sit on the surface of an object, like a balloon, and in current electricity, the particles move through a substance. They can be transferred to another object, like when you touch a doorknob after walking across a carpeted floor.

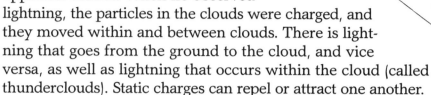

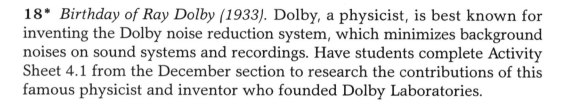

People can see electricity around them in many ways. Franklin saw electricity through lightning. He helped us understand how particles are charged negatively and positively, and how opposites attract. When he observed lightning, the particles in the clouds were charged, and they moved within and between clouds. There is lightning that goes from the ground to the cloud, and vice versa, as well as lightning that occurs within the cloud (called thunderclouds). Static charges can repel or attract one another.

18* *Birthday of Ray Dolby (1933).* Dolby, a physicist, is best known for inventing the Dolby noise reduction system, which minimizes background noises on sound systems and recordings. Have students complete Activity Sheet 4.1 from the December section to research the contributions of this famous physicist and inventor who founded Dolby Laboratories.

19 *Birthday of James Watt, inventor of the steam engine (1736).*

19* *Invention of storing and preserving foods in the tin can by Ezra Daggett and Thomas Kensett (1825).* Activity Sheet 5.6 helps students understand the nature of storing foods and other preservation methods. It is helpful to talk to the students about proper food storage, including the length of time to store foods, how to recognize if foods are spoiled regardless of preservation method (depressed tin can lids), and methods of preservation, including canning, freezing, wrapping, and labeling of foods. For more on food preservation, students can refer to Activity 9.5 (in May–June) on pickling or to Activity 4.2 (in December).

21 *Birthday of John Fitch, steamboat developer (1743).*

24* *Gold discovered at Sutter's Mill in California (1848).* This discovery led to the 1849 Gold Rush. See Activity Sheet 5.7. Students can learn more about the history of mining and the Gold Rush when people headed west to find gold. Identification of true gold versus iron pyrite, known as *fool's gold,* is something that students might enjoy learning more about. You can talk to your students about the value of gold and how it changes, as well as the amount of gold in different objects with which they are familiar; examples are the quality of gold in jewelry (for example, ten carat versus eighteen carat) and gold plating. In Activity Sheet 5.7, students will examine different minerals for their hardness and identification purposes.

25* *Birthday of Robert Boyle, Irish scientist (1627).* Boyle published a book in 1660 relating to the pressure of a gas, which he called "the spring of air." He experimented with mercury and test tubes measuring the amount of trapped air in the tubes and the height of the levels of mercury. His findings, called Boyle's law, explain that air volume can be measured and air pressure can change. What he found is that volume decreases as air pressure increases, which is an inverse proportion in scientific terms. Boyle also considered the temperature of the air and the mass of the gas, which explains that gas is affected by temperature and pressure. There are exceptions to Boyle's law, when gases are at either extremely low temperature or very high pressure, but generally his early findings have helped us understand air and gases. See Activity Sheet 5.8. For background information on Boyle, visit this Web site: www.bbk.ac.uk/boyle/biog.html.

25* *U.S. transcontinental telephone service began from New York to California (1915).* This historic telephone conversation was between Alexander Graham Bell and Thomas A. Watson. Use Activity Sheet 5.9 to make mini-phones and learn more about how sound travels.

27* *Birthday of Wolfgang Mozart (1756).* Learn more about sound with Activity Sheet 5.3.

28* *First commercial telephone switchboard operated (1878).* This is a good time to relate the month's progression in activities understanding sound and how it travels. Use Activity 5.9.

Activity Sheet 5.1.

Can Molecules Move?

Materials

3 average-sized balloons   3 empty soda bottles

elastic bands   3 bowls or plastic dishpans

hot water   cold water

lukewarm water   ice cubes

Procedure

1. Fit the three balloons over the mouths of the three bottle openings. Use elastic bands to secure the necks of the bottles so that air cannot escape.

2. Put hot tap water in one dishpan, lukewarm in another, and cold water with ice in the third. **Be careful with the hot water!**

3. Set the bottles with the balloons attached in each of the three pans of water. Observe what happens to each balloon.

Conclusions

1. What happened to each of the three balloons?

2. Did the temperature of the water have an effect on this?

3. What can you say about the molecules of air inside the balloon?

For Further Study

Read about hot-air balloons. How are they operated? What makes them rise into the air? How are they controlled while in the air? How do they descend?

   Write a mini-report and use the illustration on the next page as your report's cover. Color it if desired.

(TITLE)

(NAME)   (DATE)

146

Activity Sheet 5.2.

Colossal Comets

For more than five hundred years, comets have been observed and charted as they orbit Earth. Have you ever seen a picture of a comet with a tail? The sun causes the ice at the nucleus of a comet to turn to vapor, and creates a *coma,* which is composed of dust, water, vapor, and gas. Comets actually have two tails: one composed of a gas and one of glowing charged gas.

Find out about comets that have come near or even hit Earth. To gather information and better understand comets, visit these three Web sites:

www.windows.ucar.edu/tour/link=/comets/comets.html

www.nineplanets.org/comets.html

www.nasm.si.edu/research/ceps/etp/comets

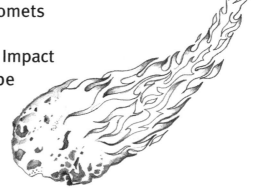

Any special NASA launches like the Deep Impact spacecraft on January 12, 2005, should be included in your report. Can you find information on dinosaur extinction by comets?

Use the information you learned in your research to complete the chart that follows.

Date	Event	Source of Information	Results or Information Discovered

Did You Hear That? Detecting Differences in Pitch

Vocabulary		
amplitude	wavelength	pitch

Materials

4 drinking glasses of same size and height

water

pencil

Procedure

1. Fill three glasses with water at different levels. Leave one glass empty.
2. Gently tap the pencil on each glass rim to create sounds.
3. Listen to each of the four glasses, and note the differences in sound.
4. Arrange the glasses in order from lowest to highest sounds or pitch.

Here's What You're Hearing:

Sound, like light, travels in waves. You hear different types of soundwaves as different sounds.

- High-pitched sounds have short wavelengths, like this:
  Each wave is this long:
- Low-pitched sounds have longer wavelengths, like this:
  Each wave is this long:
- Loud sounds have wavelengths with greater amplitude than quiet sounds:
  LOUD: QUIET:
  Amplitude

Did You Hear That? Detecting Differences in Pitch *(Cont'd.)*

Visit these Web sites to understand sound waves and pitches: www.glenbrook.k12.il.us/gbssci/phys/Class/sound/U11l2c.html and www.fi.edu/fellows/fellow2/apr99/soundvib.html.

Conclusions

1. Which glass had the highest pitch? The lowest pitch?
2. Describe the pitch of the empty glass.
3. Why does the pitch change?

For Further Study

Read about Stephen Foster and Wolfgang Mozart. Write a mini-report about their lives and contributions. Then complete the following chart.

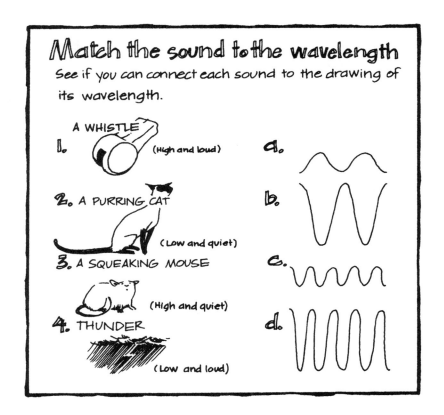

Activity Sheet 5.4.

Understanding the Properties of Oil

Have you ever heard it said that oil and water don't mix? To learn more about the concepts behind this phrase, visit this Web site: www.library.thinkquest. org/J001539/exp1.html.

If we do mix oil and water, such as in salad dressing, and the mixture is left undisturbed, we see that the oil and vinegar (which is mostly water) separate. What about an oil spill in the ocean? What happens to the oil?

The molecules of water and oil are different. In chemistry, the term *miscible* refers to the property of various liquids that allows them to be mixed together. Because oil is made up of carbon, hydrogen, oxygen, and other atoms, and water is made up of two atoms of hydrogen and one of oxygen, they are *immiscible,* which means that they cannot be mixed together.

Try this experiment to make an *emulsion,* a special mixture of oil and water that stays mixed, for example, mayonnaise.

Understanding the Properties of Oil *(Cont'd.)*

Materials

2-cup glass measuring cup

½ cup of water

½ cup of oil

2-cup glass jar with lid

½ teaspoon of liquid detergent

Procedure

1. Pour ½ cup of water into the 2-cup glass measuring cup.
2. Pour ½ cup of oil on top.
3. Watch the oil and water separate.
4. Leave the container alone for 5 minutes
5. Pour the contents into the glass jar and seal with the lid.
6. Shake well and observe the mixture. Describe what you observe.
7. Wait at least 1 hour. Then come back and observe the mixture again.
8. Now add the detergent, and shake the contents of the jar well.
9. Leave the contents in the jar and observe in 5 minutes.

Conclusions

1. What happened to the mixture after you shook it in the jar?
2. What happened after you left the mixture for 1 hour?
3. What happened when you added the detergent to the mixture? Why?

151

Can Electrons Transfer from One Object to Another?

Materials

2 balloons   ruler

2 yards of thread   scissors

tape   piece of wool

Procedure

1. Blow up the balloons and knot them at the ends. Cut the piece of thread in half.

2. Tie one piece of thread to the knot at the end of one balloon and the other piece to the knot at the end of the other balloon.

3. Tape the ends of the threads from both balloons to the same end of the ruler (see the illustration).

4. Have a partner hold the ruler steadily so that the balloons are free to dangle. Observe what happens to the two balloons as they are held steadily.

5. Now take the piece of wool (it could be part of your clothing). Rub it against the balloons for about half a minute, and then let go of the balloons. What happens to them?

6. Visit these two Web sites to understand static electricity and electron transfer: www.enchantedlearning.com/physics/staticelectricity.shtm/ and www.sciencemadesimple.com/static.html.

Can Electrons Transfer from One Object to Another? *(Cont'd.)*

Conclusions

1. What happens to the electrons on your piece of wool when you rub it against the balloon? Where do they go?

2. What does this do to the balloons? How are they charged (positively or negatively) once they acquire the extra electrons? Do they have the same attraction?

Here's another example of electron transfer:

Have you ever gotten a shock when you're in your stocking feet and you touch something made of metal? This happens because you have transferred some of your electrons through your feet to the surface you are standing on. This makes you positively charged. When you touch something (like metal) that conducts electrons easily — that is, something that readily transfers electrons — you pick up electrons and get a shock.

Think, Read, Find Out!
Why are you more likely to get a shock when you don't have your shoes on?

Activity Sheet 5.6.

Ways to Preserve Foods

To learn more about ways to preserve foods, visit this informational Web site before you begin the activity: www.canning-food-recipes.com/canning.htm.

Materials

1 package of fruit pectin

1- or 2-cup glass or plastic container with tight-fitting lid

recipe for no-cook freezer jams (see the pectin package for the recipe)

4 cups of sugar

lemon juice (see the recipe for the exact amount)

fresh fruit (for example, 1 quart of strawberries)

ladle or large spoon

refrigerator

Ways to Preserve Foods *(Cont'd.)*

Procedure

Follow the directions for no-cook freezer jams found on the fruit pectin box's insert.

Conclusions

1. Discuss the proper ways of preserving foods like fruits and vegetables. Compare with December's discussion of proper freezing techniques.

2. Discuss ways of using lids and freezing containers to freeze foods.

3. Compare today's plastic containers with yesterday's early freezing and food preservation techniques (for example, tin cans were used to store food in the early 1800s). Then distribute the two worksheets here.

4. Allow the children to sample the jam before freezing it. After three weeks, sample the jam again, and discuss how it tasted before freezing and how it tasted after freezing.

After reading on the web about today's proper food storage, list three ways in which modern can storage is similar to the technique first used in 1825.

1. _____
_____
_____
_____

2. _____
_____
_____
_____

3. _____
_____
_____
_____

early tin
can storage
by Donkin, Hall
& Gamble, 1825.

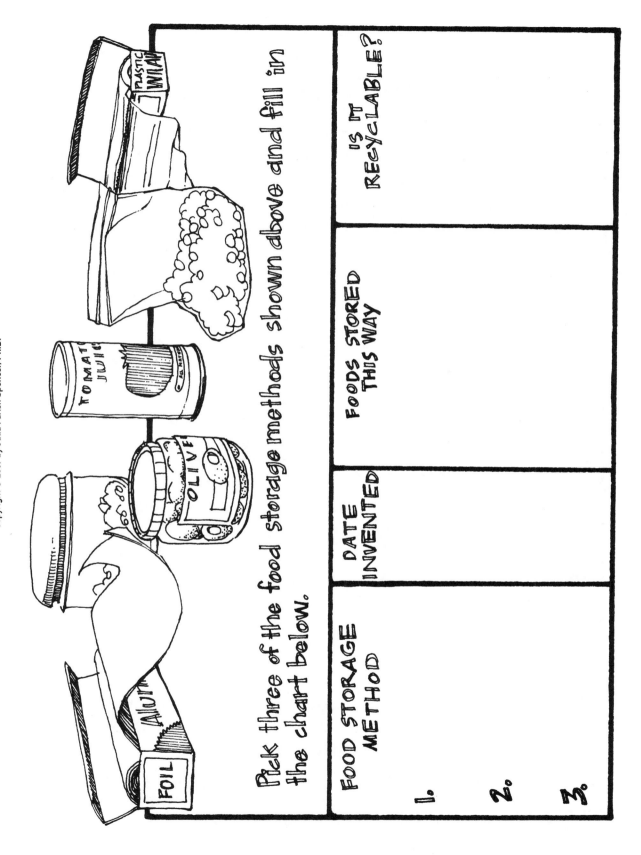

Pick three of the food storage methods shown above and fill in the chart below.

FOOD STORAGE METHOD	DATE INVENTED	FOODS STORED THIS WAY	IS IT RECYCLABLE?
1.			
2.			
3.			

Activity Sheet 5.7.

The World of Minerals

Minerals are natural elements formed through geological processes that can be found throughout the planet Earth. In 1812, German mineralogist Friedrich Mohs created a hardness scale that measures the scratch resistance of a mineral based on the ability of a harder mineral to scratch a softer mineral without breaking. The scale is measured from 1 to 10, with 1 being the softest and 10 being the hardest.

Hardness is one measure of the strength of a mineral's structure. Generally minerals with small atoms packed tightly together are harder than minerals with larger atoms loosely connected to one another.

For this activity, you will study the properties of three common minerals and test their hardness.

Caution: Adult supervision is required for scratching the samples with a knife.

Materials

quartz

pyrite

mica

penny

knife

Procedure

1. Carefully examine the three mineral samples, and look at the differences among them. You will be filling out the chart in the Conclusion, so look at it now to see the information required.

2. Number your samples from one to three or by name. Then describe the colors found in each sample, and record the information on the chart. Describe any streaks found, and record the information. If luster is present, enter and describe that information. Is your mineral shiny or dull?

158

The World of Minerals *(Cont'd.)*

3. Perform three tests for hardness. (a) Use your fingernail to try to scratch each sample. What are the results? (b) Repeat this test with a penny. Can you see the scratch mark from a penny? (c) Now try the test with a knife **with the supervision of an adult.** Record in the chart under "Results of Hardness Test" which scratches were obvious: those of the fingernail, penny, or knife.

MOHS'S hardness scale		
Hardness	**Mineral**	
1	**TALC** (used in talcum powder and chalk)	
2	**GYPSUM** (used in cement and plaster)	
3	**CALCITE**	
4	**FLUORITE** (used in opalescent glass and camera lenses)	
5	**APATITE** (found in our teeth)	
6	**ORTHOCLASE FELDSPAR** (used in porcelain)	
7	**QUARTZ**	
8	**TOPAZ** (commonly used in jewelry)	
9	**CORUNDUM** (rubies and sapphires)	
10	**DIAMOND**	

The World of Minerals *(Cont'd.)*

Conclusion

Complete the chart, and discuss your findings with your classmates.

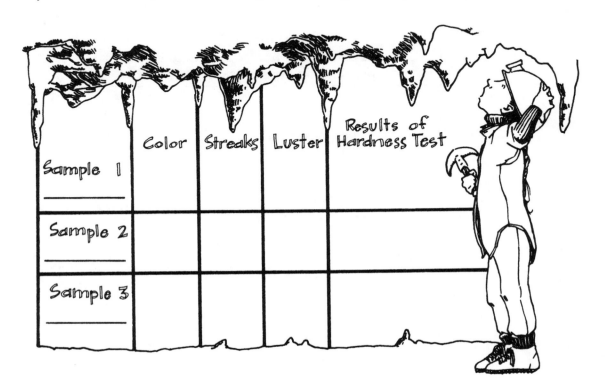

	Color	Streaks	Luster	Results of Hardness Test
Sample 1 _____				
Sample 2 _____				
Sample 3 _____				

For Further Study

Read about the California Gold Rush in the nineteenth century. What is the difference between gold and fool's gold? What is iron pyrite? Can you find two Web sites to reference that you would recommend? List their Web site addresses (their URLs) below and describe why you liked these sites.

_____

_____

_____

_____

Activity Sheet 5.8.

Molecular Bon Voyage?

Materials

sturdy empty bottle with cork stopper

funnel

bottle of distilled vinegar

teaspoon

box of baking soda

Procedure

Warning: This procedure is to be done only by an adult.

1. Put the funnel into the neck of the empty bottle. Pour about ¾ inch of vinegar into the bottle. Rinse and dry the funnel before adding the baking soda.

2. Put about 1 to 1½ teaspoons of baking soda into the bottle. Remove the funnel, and carefully put the cork back into the bottle.

3. **Warning:** Everyone stands away from the bottle to observe the reaction.

Conclusions

1. What happens to the cork and why?

2. The gas that forms inside the bottle is carbon dioxide. What happens to the molecules of gas?

For Further Study

Have students read and find out about Boyle and Boyle's law. They can use the form on the next page for their reports. A useful Web site to visit is www.bbk.ac.uk/boyle/biog.html.

Name: _____

FOR FURTHER STUDY
Read about Robert Boyle
and his theory of gas
(Boyle's law).

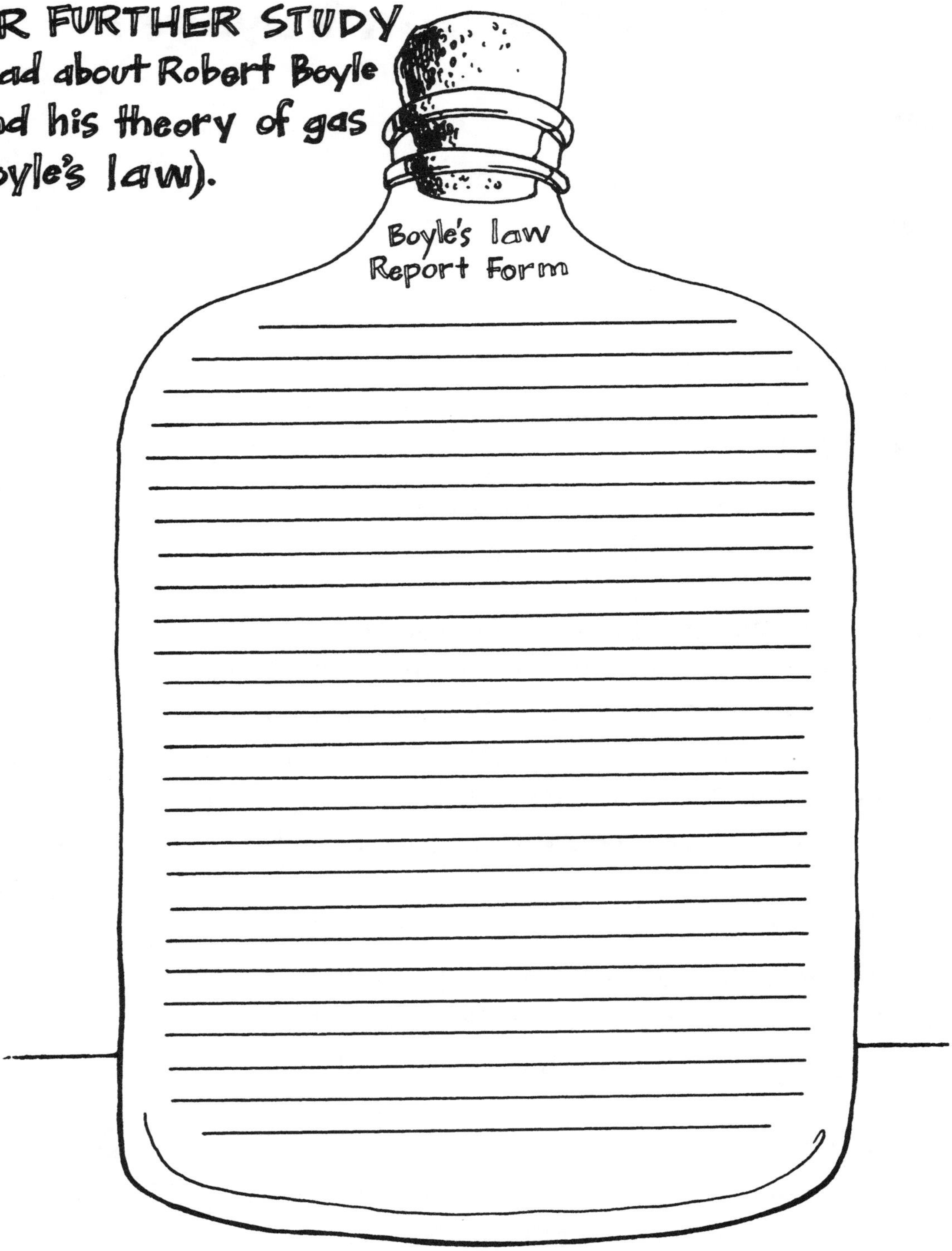

Boyle's law
Report Form

Write what you find out in the report form above.

Activity Sheet 5.9.

How Does Sound Travel?

This activity will give you the chance to learn about sound and its vibrations.

Materials

2 tin cans that are the same size, with lids removed

hammer and nail

scissors

ball of cotton string

wax

tape

buttons

paper and markers

Procedure to Make a Mini-Phone

1. Cut a length of string 3 feet long.
2. Your teacher will hammer the nail into the cans to make one hole in the bottom of each that is big enough to thread the string through.
3. Thread the string through the two holes and make a knot at each end of the cans to secure the string. As always, be cautious about any ragged edges around the holes in the cans.
4. Decorate the cans with paper and markers.
5. Work in pairs to talk through these mini-phones. Pull the cords taut and experiment with sound vibrations and relaying messages back and forth.

Visit this Web site for further information: www.iit.edu/~smile/ph9110.html.

How Does Sound Travel? *(Cont'd.)*

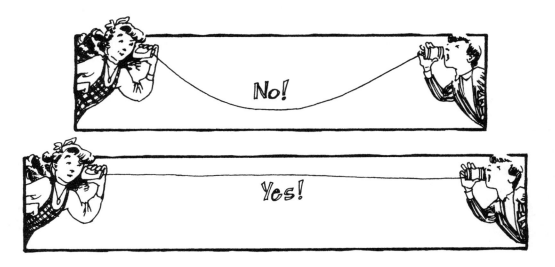

Conclusion

How is sound carried from one can to the other? What happens? Why do you think this works?

For Further Study

Read about Alexander Graham Bell and his invention of the telephone. You can also do a Web search using the key words "Alexander Graham Bell," and write down a few facts that you learn. Be sure to visit a few sites, and record the online Web address for the site you liked best. Explain why you thought it was best.

Use the following worksheet to draw a picture of a telephone of the future, and tell what this phone will do.

How Does Sound Travel? *(Cont'd.)*

Alexander Graham Bell's first
telephone transmitter and receiver

The phone of the future
designed by: _____

JANUARY

1 Find out about this famous Midnight Rider whose horseback ride in 1775 made quite a difference in many people's lives. Look for more in January Trivia.

2

3

4 Who was Sir Isaac Newton? Why was he famous? Read about him and write a biographical sketch on your form for January.

5 Let's learn about hot-air balloons using Activity Sheet 5.1.

6

JANUARY

7 Find out about early balloon flights. Your teacher will tell you about what happened today in 1785, or play January Trivia to learn more.

8

9

10 Happy Birthday, Norman George Heatley. Use Activity Sheet 1.10 or Activity Sheet 4.1 to learn more about Heatley and penicillin.

11

12 NASA's Deep Impact Spacecraft launched in 2005. Find out about comets with Activity Sheet 5.3.

JANUARY

13 A famous composer was born today. Who? January Trivia will tell all. Have fun detecting different ranges in pitch. Use Activity Sheet 5.2.

14 Happy Birthday, David Wesson. Use Activity Sheet 5.4 to learn about oil and water mixing. Also, dinosaur-eating mammals are discovered in China. (2005)

15

16

17 Never fly a kite in a storm, even on Ben Franklin's birthday. In fact, go indoors when there is lightning. Use Activity Sheet 5.5 to learn more about static electricity.

18 Happy Birthday, Ray Dolby. Use Activity Sheet 4.1 to learn more about Ray Dolby.

JANUARY

19 Who invented the steam engine? January Trivia will tell. Have fun making preserved jam, using Activity Sheet 5.6.

20

21 Play January Trivia to learn about steamboat developer John Fitch. You may want to do a mini-report on steamboats. How do they operate?

22

23 A hidden signature on this page tells who was born today.

24 Gold was discovered in California today in 1848. What does January Trivia tell you about "gold"? Use Activity Sheet 5.7 to learn more about minerals.

JANUARY

25 Your teacher has a special demonstration for you today. Use Activity Sheet 5.8.

26 Name the state to the right that celebrates its statehood today. What are some of its resources and products? Use your mini-report to record the information you find.

27 A famous composer, Wolfgang Mozart, was born today in 1756. Do Activity Sheet 5.2 if you haven't already, and listen to a recording of Mozart's creations.

28 Invent a phone of the future using Activity Sheet 5.9. Talk about the developments in telephones since the first commercial switchboard opened today in 1878.

29

30/31

February

February is an appropriate month to teach a unit on animals, beginning with Groundhog Day on February 2. Students can learn about mammals like the groundhog and how their life is affected and determined by environmental conditions such as lack of food and extremely cold weather during the winter.

This month offers the chance to learn about the fauna of different regions of North America, comparing, for example, animals that live in the desert with those that live in woodlands and mountains.

Although other topics are addressed this month, the focus is on animals, including some specific differences between warm- and cold-blooded animals and the influence of the environment on animal adaptation and survival.

Some February Dates to Remember and Background Information for the Activities

Activity sheets are provided for starred dates only. It is your decision whether to give the students facts on each entry. And for the trivia game referred to, go to Appendix 5.

1 *First motion picture studio (1893).* Another successful invention of Thomas Edison (see December 31), the first motion picture studio was established in West Orange, New Jersey, on this date.

2* *Groundhog Day.* German settlers in and around Pennsylvania brought this legend, which dates back to Roman times and Candlemas Day, to North America and selected the woodchuck (groundhog) as a prognosticator of spring. In parts of Europe, a badger was selected as the prognosticator. Since 1887, Groundhog Day has been marked on our calendars as the day to visit Punxsutawney Phil in Punxsutawney, Pennsylvania. (See Appendix 2 for book information.) Visit the Web site www.groundhogs.com for more information.

The groundhog is a hibernating mammal that prepares for hibernation early in the summer by cleaning and fixing its winter home and feasting to almost double its normal weight. This is an important natural process, as the stored fat makes it possible for the groundhog to survive during the cold months when no food is available and it is hibernating. During the state of hibernation, the groundhog goes through certain physiological changes, including a drop in heartbeat from eighty beats per minute to four or five beats per minute.

Activity Sheet 6.1 helps students understand hibernation. Students are encouraged to read about the hibernation habits of several different animals and report on one of them using the outline provided.

Be sure that students understand that the environment can affect an animal's growth and development, especially when there is a shortage of food, shelter, sunlight, and changes in temperature. Also, as they will see in other activities in February, lack of water can affect the animal's general development and survival. Another Web site the students can visit is www.sciencemadesimple.com/animals.html.

All animals carry out routine tasks to survive, including building nests or burrows or dens, preparing for changes in the seasons or weather, looking for food, and eating.

Shadow Game: You may want to play a shadow game with your students. Have them cut out small shapes of the animals they are researching and glue the shape of the animal on a tongue depressor or ice cream stick. Then project the image of the animal in front of a light onto a screen. Students can guess which animal's shadow is being projected. You may also want to reinforce the fact that shadows can change in size. The opaque animal held in front of a projector light is a good stimulus for discussion on shadows. Students may want to follow up by measuring their own shadows at different times of the day.

3 *Birthday of Spencer Fullerton Baird (1823).* Baird, an American naturalist and zoologist, is credited with developing the Smithsonian Institution in Washington, D.C., into a national treasure. This is a good time of the year to visit a museum and its collections, especially a museum's artifacts. By the end of his tenure as secretary of the museum, Baird had collected and displayed more than 2.5 million items.

Have the students write a mini-report on Baird using the form in Appendix 6 of this book. Also, have students bring in a display of science items to the classroom, and set up your own mini-science museum. You could invite guest speakers, like a naturalist or a zoologist, and learn more about mammals and birds through their presentations. Many are willing to bring live specimens to your classroom.

You may also want to build a bird house as a project and have students feed the birds as part of the project. Winter is a good time of the year in many communities to feed birds and observe their behaviors. Of course, once you start feeding them during the winter, it is imperative that you continue to provide food for them during the colder winter months. Students can observe different types of birds and their beaks, so they will better understand adaptation as well.

4 Apollo 14 *landed on the moon (1971).* *Apollo 14* astronauts Alan Shepard and Edgar Mitchell landed on the moon, while astronaut Stuart Roosa stayed in orbit around the moon. The flight had been launched on January 31.

4* *Birthday of Clement Ader (1841).* Ader was an inventor, and among his many inventions, one in particular is noteworthy this month. Based on his observations of bats and their flight patterns, he created a steam-powered aircraft called the *Eole* and made its wings in the shape of a bat's wings (the first batmobile!).

Students may be fascinated to learn more about Ader. You can stress how many scientists have used the observation of animals, such as the flight patterns of birds and mammals, in thinking up their inventions. Students may also want to read about bats and what fascinating creatures they are.

Have students report on Ader using the Who's Who in Science form in Appendix 6. Students can also do September's Activity Sheet 1.3, Patent an Invention, or Activity Sheet 6.3, In Honor of National Inventor's Day, and create an invention for a science project, perhaps with an emphasis on animals and animal behavior.

Teachers can also build a bat house for their students and place it on school grounds if permissible. Check out these sites for instructions and information on building a bat house:

www.batcon.org/bhra/economyhouse.html

www.nwf.org/backyardwildlifehabitat/bathouse.cfm

www.dfw.state.or.us/springfield/bat_houses.html

Building and placing a bat house will require teacher supervision.

5* *National Wildlife Federation founded (1936).* Activity Sheet 6.2 encourages students to use one of the fine publications of the National Wildlife Federation, such as *Ranger Rick* (for ages 6 to 12). Students will create a wildlife notebook based on a choice from one of five categories of vertebrates.

Student research and reports should stress environmental factors that influence animal behavior and adaptation. Visit the National Wildlife Federation's Web sites at www.nwf.org and www.nwf.org/kids.

8* *Birthday of Henry Walter Bates (1825).* Bates, a British naturalist and explorer, is credited with first describing animal mimicry, where animals copy or mimic the coloring or behavior of another animal in the same species. He mostly studied mimicry among butterflies. For more information on butterfly mimicry, visit this site: www.home.cogeco.ca/ ~lunker/ mimicry.htm. Have students complete the Biographical Sketch form in Appendix 6 of this book. They can also go on the Internet or to the library and read about animal mimicry, then do a report or poster for the class on their findings.

This can lead to a discussion of biodiversity and natural selection and how species of animals survive. Children may be amazed to learn that there are two thousand kinds of fireflies. Before starting these activities, discuss the information provided on fireflies, or have the children read about them. Then have the students use the template to create their own trivia questions and answers, using the Plants and Animals card in Appendix 5. Have them work in groups and predict the number of species of fireflies and the number of species of certain types of animals, and then do research to see how accurate their predictions were.

9 *First official forecast made by U.S. Weather Bureau (1870).* You may want your students to discuss the forecasting abilities of animals. How are they able to detect weather changes, and how do they adapt to weather conditions?

11 *The space shuttle* Challenger *returned to Earth after the first untethered spacewalk (1983).*

11* *National Inventor's Day.* Talk about inventions the students could create (perhaps only in their words or imagination). Think about inventions for animals. Then use Activity Sheet 6.3 to celebrate National Inventor's Day. Students can also use September's Activity Sheet 1.3, Patent an Invention. Visit the Web at homeschooling.about.com/library/blfeb11a.htm.

11 *Birthday of Thomas Edison (1847).* This is a good time to have your students write a mini-report about one of Edison's inventions or a biography sketch using the forms found in Appendix 6.

12 *Birthday of Abraham Lincoln (1809).*

12* *Birthday of Charles Darwin, English naturalist (1809).* Although Darwin is known primarily for formulating a theory of natural selection and evolution, he also studied earthworms. Students can investigate earthworms themselves today using Activity Sheet 6.4. Talk about how earthworms react to certain stimuli, describe their anatomy, and share with students the fascination that early scientists once shared. Earthworms may be found in your area of the country or ordered from one of the biological supply companies listed in Appendix 2. Two great earthworm Web sites are www.biologycorner.com/worksheets/earthwormdissection.htm and www.naturewatch.ca/english/wormwatch/programs/inv1.htm/.

14 *Valentine's Day.* Legend has it that birds choose their mates today. You may want to ask students about this myth. Certain migratory birds will be making their return journeys north in the next six weeks and soon after they return, they select their mates.

14* *Arizona admitted to the Union (1912).* Activity Sheet 6.5 takes students to the desert in their investigation of animals and their habitats. Have them visit these two Web sites: www.desertusa.com/animal.html and www.enchantedlearning.com/biomes/desert/desert/shtm/.

15 *Galileo was born (1564).* Perhaps you will want your students to read and report on this famous Italian astronomer. They can use the Biographical Sketch form in Appendix 6.

18 *Planet Pluto discovered (1930).* Talk to your students about this planet, and have them write mini-reports on it. What are conditions like on Pluto? Could animals and plants survive there? What data support their conclusions? How did the pioneering work of early astronomers such as Galileo help pave the way to discovering Pluto? Might Pluto not even be a planet?

19 *Birthday of Nicolaus Copernicus (1473).* The father of astronomy was born on this day. Have your students visit the Web for biographical information and use the form in Appendix 6 to write a mini-report about him. Today we have powerful telescopes that can see deep into space, but Copernicus used his naked eye for many of his observations.

22 *Birthday of George Washington (1732).*

24 *Birthday of Steve Jobs (1955).* Steve Jobs is the CEO of Apple, which he cofounded in 1976, and Pixar, the Academy Award–winning animation studios that he cofounded in 1986. Apple launched the personal computer revolution in the 1970s with the Apple II and reinvented the landscape in the 1980s with the Macintosh. Today, Apple is known for its innovative and award-winning technology for many things, from computers to iPods. For more information, visit www.apple.com/pr/bios/jobs.html. Have your students research how his position as CEO of Apple and also his animation studios have made significant contributions to technology.

26* *Grand Canyon National Park established (1919).* Have any of your students been to this national park? Activity Sheet 6.6 will help them investigate some of the animals that live there. They should first read more about the animals and the Grand Canyon at these two sites: www.nps.gov/grca/grandcanyon/quicklook/animalsandplants.htm and www.nationalgeographic.com/grandcanyon/kids.html and then fill out their mini-report forms found in Appendix 6. There are also some recommended DVDs and videos listed in Appendix 3.

28* *Colorado admitted to the Union (1861).* Activity Sheet 6.7 presents animals that burrow underground. Which ones can be found in Colorado? Have students find out about this state. What is the state animal? Have the students read and report using the mini-report form in Appendix 6.

Two good reference Web sites are www.dnr.state.il.us/lands/education/kids/diggers.htm and www.enchantedlearning.com/coloring/underground.shtm/.

29* *The extra day for leap year (just in case)!* Leap year occurs every fourth year (except in years ending in 00, unless divisible by 400; thus, 1600 and 2000 were leap years—but 1700, 1800, and 1900 were not). To figure out if a non–00 year is a leap year, divide the year by 4. Whether it's actually a leap year or not, your students may enjoy trying this mathematical challenge in Activity Sheet 6.8 to determine when a leap year occurs. A good leap year Web site is www.timeanddate.com/date/leapyear.html.

How Long Will It Sleep?

Read and find out about hibernation. Then select one or two mammals from the list in the Word Box and read and report about that mammal's unique hibernation pattern. Be prepared to discuss your findings with your classmates. Visit www.sciencemadesimple.com/animals.html and www.groundhogs.com for more information.

Be sure to read about your mammal's physiological changes in (1) body temperature, (2) heart rate, and (3) body metabolism, including changes in body weight. Use the outline on the next page to organize your findings.

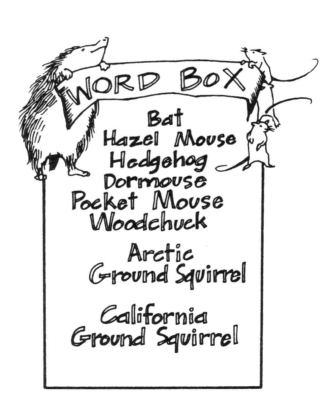

WORD BOX
Bat
Hazel Mouse
Hedgehog
Dormouse
Pocket Mouse
Woodchuck

Arctic
Ground Squirrel

California
Ground Squirrel

Hibernation of Mammals

I. Definition of hibernation

    A. Reasons for hibernation

    B. Different methods of hibernation

        1. Variations among species

        2. Definition of warm-blooded animals

        3. Examples of hibernating mammals

    C. Choice of mammal for research; reasons for selection

II. Seasonal adaptation of mammal selected

    A. Summer preparation of mammal

        1. Changes in weight

        2. Natural eating patterns and diet prior to hibernation

        3. Natural enemies

    B. Fall preparation of mammal

        1. Preparation of home (burrow, den)

        2. Time of entry into hibernation

    C. Winter pattern

        1. Changes in body temperature

        2. Changes in circulation and heart rate

        3. Changes in metabolism, weight, food consumption

    D. Spring pattern

        1. Approximate time (month) of awakening

        2. Reasons for awakening

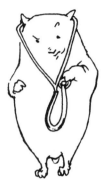

Making a Wildlife Notebook

The National Wildlife Federation was founded on February 5, 1936. How old is it now? What does it do? Have you read any of its publications? On the back of this paper, list any that you have looked at or read.

For this project, you will be creating your own wildlife notebook or scrapbook. It should have pictures (photographs or drawings) of animals that interest you. Be sure to divide your notebook into sections and plan a table of contents. Select one of these five categories for a notebook on vertebrates:

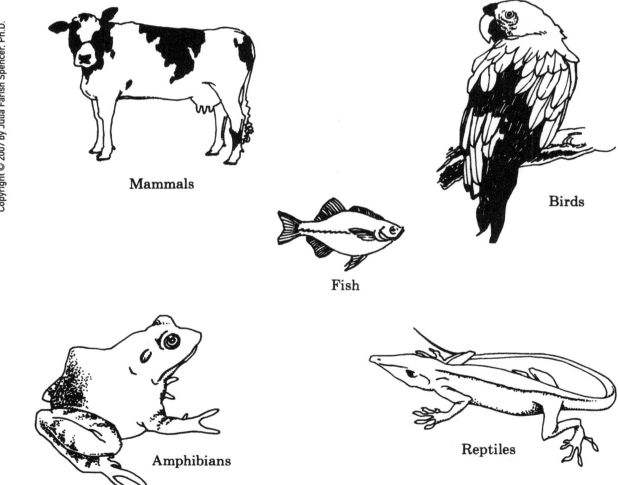

Mammals

Fish

Birds

Amphibians

Reptiles

Making a Wildlife Notebook *(Cont'd.)*

Wildlife refers to animals that can live without human intervention. See if you can find out about laws that protect wildlife. An example is laws that restrict hunting and fishing during special seasons of the year. These are ways people have attempted to help conserve wildlife and protect animals.

In your notebook, report on as many animals as you can in the category you select. Write facts that interest you. Tell about what can be done to protect the animal if you feel something needs to be done. Paste any pictures or text to your narrative report. You may want to visit these two Web sites for more information: www.nwf.org and www.nwf.org/kids.

Name _____   Date _____

In Honor of National Inventor's Day

In honor of this day, create your own invention using this form.

Use your imagination and think of an invention that would make life easier, safer, or more fun. Then answer the questions below.

Your invention's name _____

What does your invention do? _____

_____

_____

_____

_____

How would this improve life? _____

_____

_____

_____

_____

_____

_____

Name two scientists whose inventions or discoveries made your invention possible. _____

_____

_____

183

Activity Sheet 6.4.

The Earthworm

Below is a picture of an earthworm, a cold-blooded animal. Your teacher will show you the parts of an earthworm's anatomy. Use the words in the word box to label the body parts of the worm in the illustration below it. Then research earthworms in books or on the Internet, and answer the questions on the next page. Finally, complete the investigation.

Word Box

gizzard	esophagus
intestine	hearts
throat	outer segments
mouth	brain
blood vessels	pharynx
crop	

The Earthworm *(Cont'd.)*

True or False?

Write *true* or *false* to answer the following statements.

_____ 1. An earthworm has no teeth and can't chew its food.

_____ 2. The crop and gizzard help the earthworm digest its food by storing and then grinding the food. The worm swallows tiny pebbles and parts of rock that help grind the food, too.

_____ 3. The waste products of the worm that it eliminates are called "castings." These help enrich the soil.

_____ 4. The earthworm has no eyes or ears, but it can see and hear.

_____ 5. The earthworm lives in darkness and is sensitive to light.

_____ 6. The earthworm has five hearts.

_____ 7. An earthworm can live as long as a dog or a cat.

Let's Investigate

Try this investigation. Be sure to take good care of your worms and return them to the outside soil after this activity.

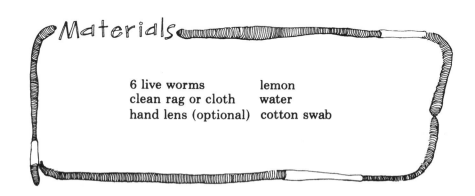

Materials

6 live worms	lemon
clean rag or cloth	water
hand lens (optional)	cotton swab

The Earthworm *(Cont'd.)*

Procedure

1. Look at your earthworms by placing them on the clean cloth or rag. Use your hand lens if desired. Observe the worms in dim light if possible.

2. Take a cotton swab, and gently touch the tip to one end of a worm. What happens?

3. Turn the worm over and look for bristles on its underside.

4. Put some fresh lemon juice on a cotton swab. Gently touch the end of the worm with the moistened cotton swab. What happens?

Conclusions

1. Based on your observations of the external anatomy of the earthworm, how does the earthworm use its bristles?

2. What did you observe about the use of light and the earthworm's reaction to light? What conclusions can you draw between the earthworm's reaction to light and its natural underground habitat where it is dark?

3. Did your earthworm react to the lemon juice? What did it do and why?

For more information about earthworms visit: www.biologycorner.com/worksheets/earthwormdissection.htm and www.naturewatch.ca/english/wormwatch/programs/inv1.html.

A Who's Who of Desert Animals

Learn about animals that live in the American desert by looking in books and on the Internet. Two desert animal Web sites to visit are www.desertusa.com/ animal.html and www.enchantedlearning.com/ biomes/desert/desert/shtm/. Find out about the weather and other conditions of the desert that affect these animals' daily lives.

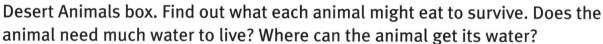

Write the correct name of each animal next to the picture in the Desert Animals box. Find out what each animal might eat to survive. Does the animal need much water to live? Where can the animal get its water?

On the Animals of the Desert report form, write a few facts about three animals of your choice from the desert animals Word Box below.

Word Box

nine-banded armadillo	gambel's quail
North American desert iguana	jackrabbit
sidewinder	kit fox
kangaroo rat	

DESERT ANIMALS

187

ANIMALS OF THE DESERT

Activity Sheet 6.6.

Animals of the Grand Canyon

All of the animals pictured in the box live in the Grand Canyon. Read the words in this Word Box, and write the correct name of the animal next to the picture of the animal shown below.

Word Box		
egret	porcupine	tassel-eared squirrel
burro	bighorn sheep	coyote
mountain lion	bobcat	

Find out about as many of these animals as you can by visiting these two Web sites for information on the Grand Canyon: www.nps.gov/grca/grand canyon/quicklook/animalsandplants.htm and www.nationalgeographic.com/ grandcanyon/kids.html. Write about what each animal might eat to survive. Then look at each animal and think about how it could defend itself or protect its young from predators. Are parts of its body used in protection? Write a brief report on each animal.

Activity Sheet 6.7.

Animals and Their Burrows

All of the animals in the Word Box live in underground homes (burrows). Some live in the woodlands, some in the desert, and some in other environments.

Think about each animal and its home and the similarities and differences in them. Read about them at these two Web sites: www.dnr.state.il.us/lands/education/kids/DIGGERS.htm and www.enchantedlearning.com/coloring/underground.shtm/.

On the next page, try to match the description of each animal with the correct picture of the animal by drawing a line from the animal to its description. Write the name of the animal at the end of the description.

Burrowing Animal Word Box

Groundhog   Prairie Dog   Bumblebee

Kangaroo Rat   Elf Owl   Earthworm

I like an underground burrow to lay my eggs. I usually lay several hundred. I am called a "queen." I am the

_____

I look like a huge hamster. I live in groups. I give a little bark, but I am not a real dog. My burrow is in the ground. It helps me stay cool during the summer and warm in the winter. I am the

_____

My burrow is in a cactus. I snuggle inside a hole in the giant desert cactus. I am noted for my keen eyesight, especially at night. I am the

_____

Of all the underground burrowers, I am supposed to be the best architect. I dig for hours, moving rocks and soil. My burrow may be twenty feet deep. I hibernate in my burrow. I am the

_____

My burrow is in the desert. I like to live alone. I look for my food at night. I like to store seeds in my home. I am noted for my jumps—up to six feet! I am the

_____

I have rings or segments on my body, and I twist and wiggle to move. I burrow deep into the ground. I need a damp environment. I am also nocturnal. I am the

_____

Activity Sheet 6.8.

Leap Year

Complete the chart below by checking off the leap years. To determine whether the year is a leap year, divide 4 into the year. If you have a remainder, it is not a leap year (see the examples at the bottom of this page). However, if the year ends in oo, divide the year by 400; if you have a remainder, it is not a leap year.

Visit this site for more information on leap year: www.timeanddate.com/date/leapyear.html.

1812 is a leap year   1911 is not

Extra Credit

Based on the current school year, determine when the next leap year will be. Record your answer here.

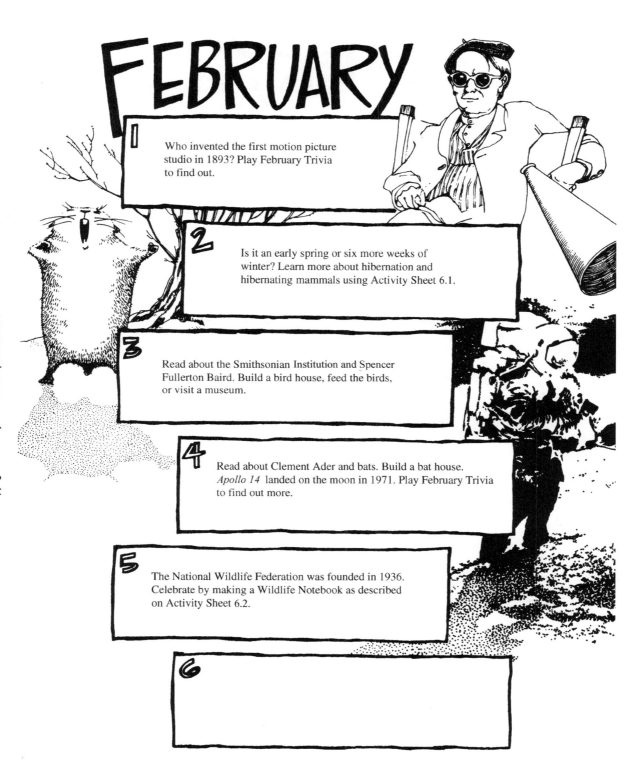

FEBRUARY

1 Who invented the first motion picture studio in 1893? Play February Trivia to find out.

2 Is it an early spring or six more weeks of winter? Learn more about hibernation and hibernating mammals using Activity Sheet 6.1.

3 Read about the Smithsonian Institution and Spencer Fullerton Baird. Build a bird house, feed the birds, or visit a museum.

4 Read about Clement Ader and bats. Build a bat house. *Apollo 14* landed on the moon in 1971. Play February Trivia to find out more.

5 The National Wildlife Federation was founded in 1936. Celebrate by making a Wildlife Notebook as described on Activity Sheet 6.2.

6

FEBRUARY

7

8

Read about Henry Walter Bates and animal mimicry.

9

U.S. Weather Bureau began today in 1870.
Record today's weather and tomorrow's forecast
on your mini-report form.

10

11

Thomas Edison was born today
in 1847. Read about him and write a
biography sketch. Create an invitation using
Activity Sheet 6.3. Play February Trivia to
find a space milestone for the U.S.

12

Let's learn about earthworms using
Activity Sheet 6.4.

Happy birthday, Abraham Lincoln!

FEBRUARY

13

14 Guess which state celebrates its statehood today? Play "A Who's Who of Desert Animals" using Activity Sheet 6.5. Happy Valentine's Day! Do you think birds really select their mates today?

NOW ENTERING ARIZONA

15 A famous astronomer named Galileo was born today in 1564. Write a biography sketch to report your research.

16

17

18 Planet Pluto was discovered on this day. Play February Trivia to find out when. Write a mini-report on Pluto.

PLUTO

NEPTUNE

URANUS

FEBRUARY

19 Famous astronomer Nicolaus Copernicus was born today in 1473. Where is Earth in its yearly journey around the sun? Can you draw a picture of its position in relation to the Sun?

20

21

22 Our first president, George Washington, was born in 1732. Read about his life and write a biographical report about him.

23

24 Birthday of Steve Jobs. Visit www.apple.com/pr/bios/jobs.html.

FEBRUARY

25

26 Grand Canyon National Park was established today in 1919. Have fun learning about some Animals of the Grand Canyon using Activity Sheet 6.6.

27

28 Colorado celebrates its statehood today. Have some matching fun using Activity Sheet 6.7 to learn about animal burrowers.

GOLD

29 Just in case it's a leap year!

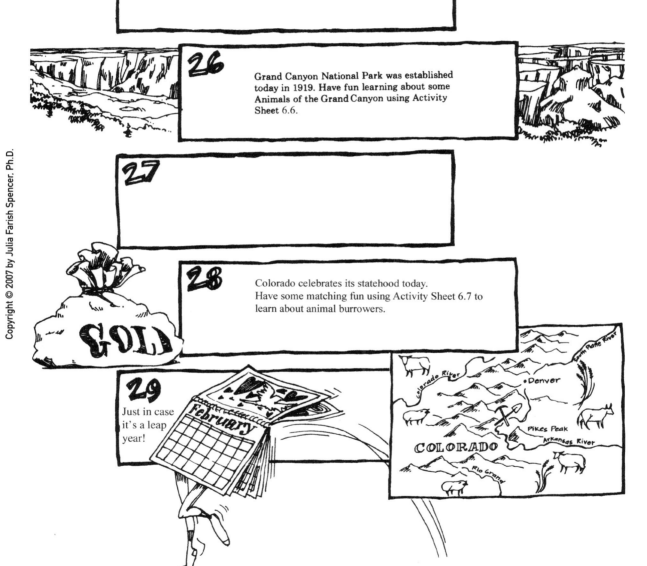

March

March is an appropriate month in which to teach a unit on plants, beginning with an investigation of the flower for March, the daffodil. Students can learn about the structure of a plant, the role of seeds and reproduction, and the differences among flowering plants.

In March we recognize the creation of two national parks: Mount Rainier and Yellowstone. This is a good time to investigate the development of seedlings and trees and to become more aware of the balance of nature, which can be disturbed by earthquake, volcanic activity, forest fires, and human destruction of flora and fauna.

Similar to February's study of animals, be sure the following concepts are presented to your students in March:

- Plants are affected by their environment, including conditions of climate and weather.
- The plant community (size and type) is influenced by the conditions of the environment, for example, desert, forest, or tropics.
- Drastic changes in the environment, for example, a drought or forest fire, may threaten the plant community.
- Successful reproductive patterns ensure plants' survival and future. Discuss pollen and seed dispersal and the structure of seeds.
- Plants and animals are interdependent. Cite examples such as the exchange of carbon dioxide and oxygen and the structure of food chains.

As in other months, there are other entries on the calendar for this month, but the ones selected for student activity sheets for March focus on plants.

Some March Dates to Remember and Background Information for the Activities

Activity sheets are provided for starred dates only. It is your decision whether to give the students facts on each entry. And for the trivia game referred to, go to Appendix 5.

1* *Daffodil, the March flower.* A jonquil (daffodil) provides a good example for looking at the parts of a flowering plant, including the ovary and the stamen, which contains the anther and the filament. This type of flower reproduces by seeds. The female part of the flower contains the stigma, the style, and the ovary (which contains the ovules). These three parts belong to the pistil. The male reproductive part consists of the stamen, which contains the anther and filament. (See Activity Sheet 7.1.) Later this month, students will investigate the apple tree, another flowering plant that produces seeds. Many plants, such as the palm tree, do not have both the male and female reproductive parts in the same flower.

Pollination occurs between plants of the same species. Pollen must move from the anther to the stigma, either within the same plant (self-pollination) or to another plant (cross-pollination). Insects, birds, and the wind can all carry pollen from one plant to another.

It is very important to understand the seed of the plant. The seed has an outer covering that protects the new plant (embryo). It also has food to feed the young embryo until it develops sufficiently to make its own food.

1* *Yellowstone National Park established (1872).* Yellowstone is located mostly in northwestern Wyoming, but it also includes narrow strips of southern Montana and eastern Idaho. (See Activity Sheet 7.2.) Encourage students to find out more about trees, especially the trees in Yellowstone and Mount Rainier National Parks.

2* *Mount Rainier National Park established (1899).* Mount Rainier National Park is located in west central Washington. (See Activity Sheet 7.2.)

3* *Florida admitted to the Union (1845).* Florida is known for its beautiful flowering plants and trees, including coconut palms. Activity Sheet 7.3 introduces students to Florida and Vermont (also admitted to the Union this month) and provides a crossword puzzle that will help students understand more about these two states. Use this opportunity to discuss seed dispersal with students. For example, the seeds of a coconut palm are often spread by wind and water. Since they are waterproof, the seeds can float on the many bodies of water found in Florida and other tropical areas and are often picked up by birds and other animals and dispersed even farther.

4* *Vermont admitted to the Union (1791).* Looking at the structure of seeds brings us to the structure of seeds like the maple tree, prominent in the northeastern states like Vermont. Activity Sheet 7.3 also examines the maple tree and its by-product, maple syrup. Vermont is famous for its maple syrup, tapped from maple trees throughout the state.

This is a good time to help students realize that trees are green plants with single stems growing to heights of ten or more feet. There are many field guides on trees, and you may want students to read and report on types of trees found in different regions of the world with different environments. Students are always interested in the unusual growth of some trees, such as the sequoia, and the differences in the shapes and appearances of trees and their leaves.

10 *First official telephone call (1876).* This historic phone call was made by Alexander Graham Bell. You may want to revisit January's Activity 5.9 regarding sound and Bell's first telephone transmitter and receiver.

11* *Johnny Appleseed Day.* In honor of nurseryman and missionary John Chapman (1774–1845), students can learn that an apple is a fruit containing the seeds of the apple tree. The apple forms a protective case around the seeds. When the apple falls from a tree or is eaten by an animal, the seeds can become scattered and dispersed, a process called *seed dispersal.*

The story of Johnny Appleseed, the real-life pioneer John Chapman, is a perfect vehicle for discussing seed dispersal and survival. It is important that each seed be dispersed or planted under conditions that will encourage its growth and development, including space away from the parent plant and other competitive trees or plants that would rob the young seedling of moisture and sunlight. See Activity Sheet 7.4.

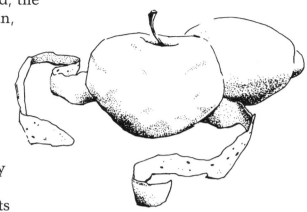

13* *Discovery of planet Uranus by Sir William Herschel (1781).* This planet is eighteen times farther from the sun than Earth is. Discuss the distance and the fact that Uranus consists of rock and layers of ice. The atmosphere consists mostly of methane gas, with some nitrogen, carbon, helium, and hydrogen. This atmosphere gives the planet a blue-green color as it absorbs red and other colors of light waves.

Students should understand that plants and animals cannot survive on planets such as Uranus because the planet cannot meet their basic needs of water, sunlight, minerals, and air. Reinforce that care of our environment and our own planet's atmosphere, soil, and water is essential to the growth and survival of plants. See Activity Sheet 7.5.

Plants and animals have a symbiotic, or mutually beneficial, relationship. Animals exhale carbon dioxide and breathe in oxygen. Plants do the opposite: they need carbon dioxide to breathe and give off oxygen. This exchange of gases between plant and animal demonstrates that respiration is essential to survival. Photosynthesis is the process by which plant cells containing chloroplasts assimilate carbon dioxide and water and produce sugar as the by-product. Light energy is essential to photosynthesis. Without it for a length of time, plants would die.

13 *Standard time adopted in the United States (1884).* Refer to October's Activity Sheet 2.11, Standard Time.

14* *Birthday of Albert Einstein (1879).* Albert Einstein was fascinated with the study of space, gravitation, and light. In 1921, he received the Nobel Prize in physics for his research. Einstein proposed that light is composed of specific quanta that are called *photons* and that light moves in wavelike patterns. He also noted that electrons were discharged when light struck certain solids.

Activity Sheet 7.6 introduces students to the fact that light has different wavelengths and amounts of energy. A prism is used to separate visible light into colors (the same as the pattern in a rainbow): red, orange, yellow, green, blue, and violet. Each color has its own wavelength and energy value. Something is blue, for example, because it absorbs the other colors and reflects blue wavelengths. Plants use this same visible light from the spectrum as energy in photosynthesis; for example, chlorophyll a and b use the energy from both red and violet lights. You may want to refer back to Activity 1.7 in Chapter One regarding refraction of light.

17* *St. Patrick's Day.* Green is a favorite on St. Patrick's Day. Objects look green because they reflect green wavelengths and absorb other colors.

The shamrock is the national flower of Ireland, and the country exports this wood sorrel species (family Oxalidaceae, the same as the pea family). The shamrock pea has pink and blue flowers and is a legume. Legumes are important to the diet of many animals, providing them protein and vitamins. There are more than ten thousand different legumes throughout the world. Peanuts, peas, and beans also belong to this family. Students will visit the Web to learn about legumes, especially alfalfa, clover, and beans, and for background information prior to completing Activity Sheet 7.7.

The shamrock was selected by St. Patrick, patron saint of Ireland in the fifth century, as a symbol of the Trinity of Christianity because it has three leaflets. The legend of St. Patrick is that he drove snakes from Ireland into the sea while carrying a shamrock as a symbol of his strong religious beliefs. On March 17, shamrocks are worn on lapels and given as gifts.

Review the information on color, shamrocks, other legumes, and St. Patrick's Day with students; then have them complete the crossword and investigation in Activity Sheet 7.7.

18 *First human walked in space (1965).* Lieutenant Colonel Aleksei A. Leonov, launched in the Soviet Union's *Voskhod 2,* was the first human to walk in space. Three months later, Edward H. White became the first American to walk in space from *Gemini-Titan 4.*

20–23* *Vernal equinox, first day of spring.* On this day, day and night are equal in length. The sun shines on the equator, and both hemispheres face and also turn away from the sun for twelve hours each. Day and night are equal everywhere on Earth on this day. (The autumnal equinox occurs between September 20 and 23.) The word *equinox* means "equal night."

On this day, the Northern and Southern Hemispheres receive the same amount of sun. In the Northern Hemisphere, the days lengthen after the vernal equinox, culminating in the longest day of the year (the first day of summer, summer solstice) around June 20 to 23.

Activity Sheet 7.8 can be used on the vernal equinox. It is a special investigation that can be done only on this day and only at the exact time of the equinox. Consult an almanac for the exact time of the equinox so that you and your students can do the activity. (Your local newspaper or television station may report the time as well.)

The activity is to have the students balance a raw egg on its narrower end at the exact time of the equinox. Some think the egg may balance at this time and not at any other due to the position of Earth in its relationship to the rotational and gravitational forces caused by the positions of Earth and the sun during the arrival of the equinox.

Since there is some controversy among scientists regarding the reliability of the "egg-speriment," have your students try it at other times and days to make their own conclusions.

23 *First manned spacecraft to change its orbital path (1965).* Virgil "Gus" Grissom and John W. Young, aboard the U.S. *Gemini-Titan 3,* were the first astronauts to change their orbital path.

24* *Agriculture Day.* Activity Sheet 7.9 introduces students to a food chain, the importance of plants to animals, and their interdependence. At the bottom of the food chain is a single green plant, a source of food for animals. Life in a drop of water reveals that microscopic animals (daphnia, or water fleas) feed on tiny plankton or green water plants. Fish feed on the fleas, birds feed on the fish, and people feed on the fish. This makes a food chain in which higher, and often more developed and larger, organisms consume smaller organisms that have fed initially on green plants.

On Agriculture Day, talk to the students about the importance of grazing for cattle and other livestock. These animals feed on grasses and sometimes legumes such as clover to enrich their diets. The larger animals are the consumers in the food chain; the tiny plants and grasses are the producers. The producers also feed on organic and inorganic matter found in the soil from dead organisms, which completes the cycle and balance in a food chain.

The humans who consume the cattle are at the top of the food chain, just as humans can be at the top of the food chain from the ocean. When food chains interconnect, they become food webs. In food webs, animals consume different sources of plants and animals; they are not dependent on only one source or system of food.

Be sure to consult Appendix 3 for correlated videos and DVDs, books, and computer programs related to the food chain.

24 *First municipality in the United States lit by electricity (1880).* Wabash, Indiana, was the first U.S. municipality to be lit by electricity.

25* *Birthday of Max Johann Sigismund Schulze (1825).* Schulze was a cytologist (a person who studies cells) and a zoologist (a person who studies animals) from Germany who is credited with discovering the protoplasm and the nucleus as parts of the cell. In both plants and animals, the cell is the fundamental building block of life. Borrow some microscopes or set up one microscope and have students take time observing the structure of a plant cell. Use the green leaf of a plant that is somewhat thin and will fit on a microscope slide. You may want to offer different types

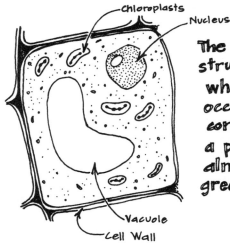

The CHLOROPLAST is the structure in plant cells where photosynthesis occurs. Chloroplasts contain CHLOROPHYLL, a pigment that gives almost all plants their green color.

of leaves to observe. Have students sketch what they see, including the nucleus and the protoplasm of the cell. In the green plants, they may also see the cell wall, cell membrane, chlorophyll in the chloroplasts, and the nucleus. Have students visit the Web reference on the Elodea, a plant: science.exeter.edu/jekstrom/WEB/CELLS/Elodea/Elodea.html.

If you want to compare plant to animal cells, have students observe cheek cells from inside the lining of their mouth (see October's Activity Sheet 2.4) and compare them to the plant cell observations. Tell the students that scientists often group plants according to their types of cells. There are singular, one-celled plants, called unicellular (plant kingdom Protista). The plant kingdom Plantae comprises mostly multicellular plants, like the red, brown, and green algae. Students can also do December's Activity Sheet 4.1 to research Schulze.

26* *German scientist Robert Koch discovered the bacterium* Bacillus, *which causes the infectious disease tuberculosis (1890).* Talk to the students about infectious diseases and how scientists make important discoveries that contribute greatly to medicine and health progress. Koch was awarded the Nobel Prize for medicine in 1905. Have students complete December's Activity Sheet 4.3, Winners of the Nobel Prize.

27* *Birthday of Karl Wilhelm von Nageli (1817).* Nageli was a Swiss botanist famous for his research on pollen and flowering plants. This month has several investigations on plants and cells, and Nageli's pioneer research paved the way for our understanding of cytoblasts in plants and chromosomes. Activity Sheet 7.7 can be used, if it was not completed on March 17. Also, students can complete the Happy Birthday Activity Sheet 7.10.

31* *Birthday of Victor Mills (1897).* This American chemical engineer spent his time working in the food and manufacturing industry, improving the quality of production for food and other products. Among his contributions, he made cake mixes less lumpy and peanut butter smoother (he perfected the process of keeping the oil from separating from the peanut butter), and he shortened the time to manufacture soap. He also invented Pampers disposable diapers. In honor of Mills, talk about science careers and applications of them in different industries. Some students have a limited view of scientists and science fields and need to broaden their understanding of how science is important in so many aspects of our world, from food to manufactured goods to medicine. January's Activity Sheet 5.4 can be used to learn about oil and separations, if it was not used in January. February's Activity Sheet 6.3 for National Inventor's Day could also be used in conjunction with this entry.

Activity Sheet 7.1.

Investigating Flowers and Their Parts

Did you know that *daffodil* is the name of a tribe of flowers belonging to the genus Narcissus? Daffodils are one of the first flowers to bloom in the spring, and they are the March Flower of the Month.

Daffodils grow from bulbs that are planted in the fall. They like soil that is well drained. In order for the flower to bloom the following year, some blossoms must be allowed to fade and the leaves to turn yellow. This gives the bulb strength for the next year's bloom.

Your teacher will show you the parts of a daffodil. Daffodils are "complete flowers" because they have four organs: sepals, petals, pistils, and stamens. It is also a "perfect flower" because it has both pistils and stamens. Look at the illustration below. Write the word from the Word Box that should go on the line next to the correct part of the flower.

Copyright © 2007 by Julia Farish Spencer, Ph.D.

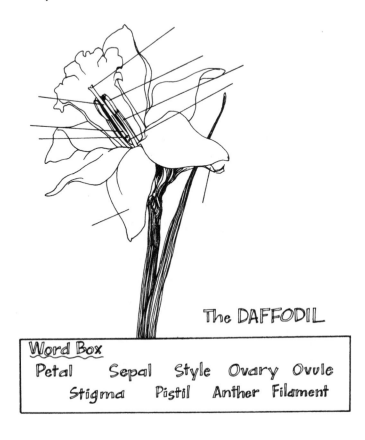

The DAFFODIL

Word Box

Petal   Sepal   Style   Ovary   Ovule

Stigma   Pistil   Anther   Filament

Investigating Flowers and Their Parts *(Cont'd.)*

For more background information on daffodils, visit www.wikipedia.org/wiki/daffodil. Daffodils have also been a source of inspiration to writers and poets. To read William Wordsworth's poem "Daffodils," visit www.bartleby.com/101/530.html.

The daffodil blooms when its reproductive organs are completely developed. The amount of sunlight is important to the time of blooming. The leaves of the daffodil contain a protein pigment that makes the plant sensitive to light. The daffodil is called a "long day" plant because it needs a long amount of sunlight—at least thirteen hours each day. Often greenhouses induce early blooming by giving the plant extra hours of artificial light.

A paper bag from the grocery store is a good cover, if the daffodil is not too big.

Try this experiment: Take two daffodils that are about to bloom. Give one of the plants a full day of sunlight. Cover the other for part of the day so that it has about half the amount of sunlight. Which one blooms first?

Read about pollination in the daffodil. Write a few facts that you discover in the Daffodil Discoveries box on the next page.

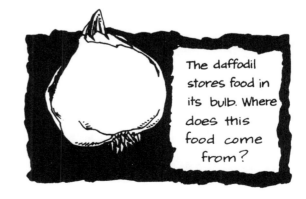

The daffodil stores food in its bulb. Where does this food come from?

209

Daffodil Discoveries:

Name _____   Date _____

Trees in Our National Parks and Around the World

Trees do not grow randomly. There are different kinds of forests in different areas of our country and around the rest of the world. Trees grow well in certain areas depending on the type of soil found there, the amount of sunlight, the climate, and the weather.

Different types of trees also have different kinds of root systems. Some roots grow very deep in the ground, whereas other types spread out just under the surface of the ground.

Spring is a good time to observe trees because it is when the tree produces its flowers. Some of the flowers are complete (male and female reproductive parts in the one tree); others are incomplete (male and female reproductive parts are in different trees).

The EUROPEAN HOP HORNBEAM has incomplete flowers also called "catkins."

QUINCE trees have complete flowers.

Trees in Our National Parks and Around the World *(Cont'd.)*

Look at the trees in your area. In the chart below, list three types of trees you observe and the date you observe each. Record any important information, for example, types of buds, dates for leaves opening, and dates for flowers blooming. Often in the spring, this can be observed in a short amount of time, perhaps a week or more; sometimes it takes longer. Pick an example that can be observed within a three-week time frame.

Date of Observation	Name of Tree	signs of BUDS	LEAVES	FLOWERS
1.				
2.				
3.				

Now read about the trees found in two famous national parks established in March: Yellowstone National Park and Mount Rainier National Park. For information on Yellowstone National Park, visit the official Web site at www.nps.gov/yell, and for more information on Mount Rainier National Park, visit the official Web site at www.nps.gov/mora. After you have read about these two parks, fill in the following page. List some of the kinds of trees in each park on a separate sheet.

212

Trees in Our National Parks and Around the World *(Cont'd.)*

Yellowstone National Park

1. I am found in three states and am the largest park in the United States. Name two of the states in which you can find me: _____ and _____.

2. I am famous for my geysers and mud volcanoes. One of my well-known geysers attracts visitors every day. It erupts about every sixty-seven minutes. What is the name of this geyser? _____

3. What is a geyser? Write a brief definition here: _____

   _____

   _____

Mount Rainier National Park

1. I am famous for a dormant volcano, ice, and glaciers. In which state am I found? _____

2. I have tree forests on my lower slopes and beautiful flowers on my mountains. List some animals that make their homes in my area. _____

   _____

   _____

   _____

3. I am found in a famous mountain range. Can you name it?

   _____

4. Here's how you can learn something about my tree seedlings. Take one seedling, plant it in soil in a jar, and water it. Cover the jar with a glass dome. Observe it the next day. What do you observe on the inside of the jar and why? _____

   _____

   _____

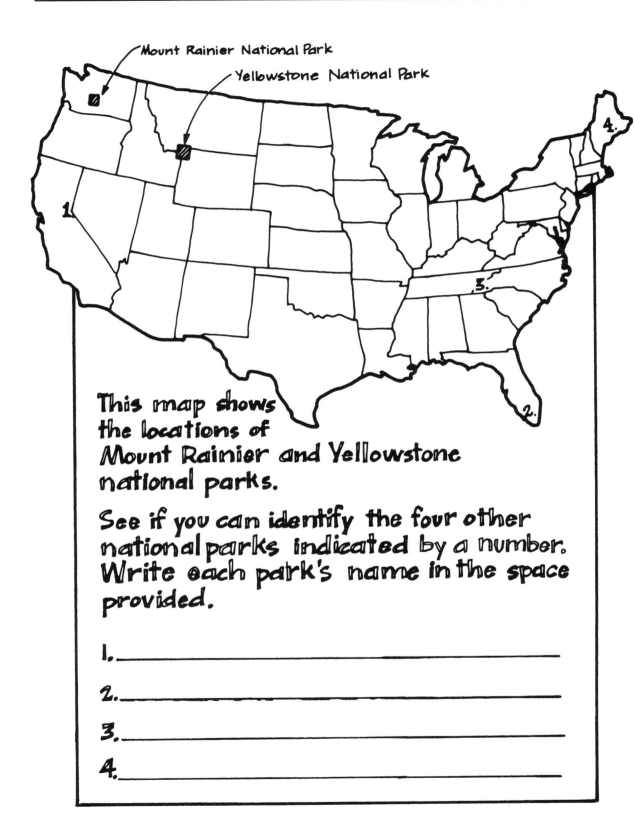

Mount Rainier National Park

Yellowstone National Park

This map shows the locations of Mount Rainier and Yellowstone national parks.

See if you can identify the four other national parks indicated by a number. Write each park's name in the space provided.

1. _____

2. _____

3. _____

4. _____

Activity Sheet 7.3.

Salutes to Florida and Vermont

Florida has more kinds of trees—over three hundred different species—than any other state. It also has many botanical gardens that draw tourists from all over the world. These sites include the famous Cypress Gardens, the Everglades National Park (which includes extremely rare species of plants found nowhere else in the world), and the J. N. "Ding" Darling National Wildlife Refuge. (Remember Ding Darling as the founder of the National Wildlife Federation?)

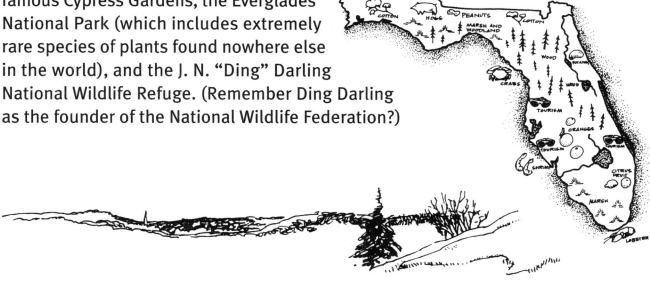

For more information on Florida, visit www.myflorida.com, and for more information on Vermont, visit www.vermont.gov/find-facts/kidspage.html.

Vermont also has a lot to boast about and to attract visitors. The famous Green Mountains, which are thick with evergreen and other trees, run through the state, making wood and paper products significant manufacturing successes.

Agriculture is also important, with symbols of the cow as reminders of the importance of dairying to the state.

215

Salutes to Florida and Vermont *(Cont'd.)*

1. During the late winter, maple farmers cut holes into the trunks of their maple trees. Buckets are hung on the trees to catch the sap that will flow out the holes during the next 4–6 weeks.

2. Maple sap is made up of a small amount of maple sugar and a lot of water. The sap is boiled in shallow pans so the water in the maple sap will evaporate.

3. The sap is then cooled. More water is allowed to evaporate away. The syrup is then bottled and enjoyed.

Maple sap is tapped from the abundant maple trees, boiled down, and sold as prized Vermont maple syrup.

One pint (or two cups) of syrup represents about twenty original cups of sap. For a recipe of homemade maple syrup and to learn how to tap maple trees for syrup, visit these two Web sites: www.mi-maplesyrup.com/Activities/activities_homemade.htm and www.umext.maine.edu/onlinepubs/PDFpubs/7036.pdf.

Salutes to Florida and Vermont *(Cont'd.)*

Across

1. I'm a type of tree found in Florida and other tropical, moist places. My leaves look like big fans. I'm related to bamboo and banana trees. I'm a _____ tree.

3. I'm a mammal with antlers and hooves. I live in forests like the Green Mountains of Vermont. I'm a _____.

4. I'm considered the "king" of the reptiles. You can visit me in Florida. I'm an _____.

8. I'm a deciduous tree with broad leaves shaped like the palm of your hand. My fruit looks like a pair of connected wings. I'm a _____ tree.

9. I'm a plant that belongs to the pineapple family. I'm grayish-green and hang from trees. Since my roots aren't in the soil and ground, I get my water from the air. I'm Spanish _____.

11. I'm the New England state famous for cows, dairy products, tree products, maple syrup, skiing, and the Green Mountains. I'm _____.

Down

2. I'm the Sunshine State. I have more than 300 different kinds of trees and more than 3,000 species of plants. I'm _____.

5. I give plants lots of energy from my light, and am important to photosynthesis. I'm _____.

6. I'm a vine that grows up a tree in tropical rain forests, but my roots are in the ground. I'm a _____ vine.

7. I'm found high in palm trees that grow in tropical areas. I have "milk" you can drink and "meat" you can eat. I have a hard, rough outer covering. I'm a _____.

10. I'm a color but I'm also the proper name of a mountain range in Vermont. I'm the _____ Mountains.

12. I'm what drips from maple trees in the early spring. After processing, I'm put on your pancakes. I'm _____.

217

Activity Sheet 7.4.

What's in an Apple?

An apple is the fruit of the apple tree. The fruit contains the seeds of the tree. Seeds can be dispersed in a variety of ways. Animals, the wind, and people (like Johnny Appleseed) are some ways that seeds are scattered so that they have a chance to develop and grow away from the parent plant, with enough space to develop on their own.

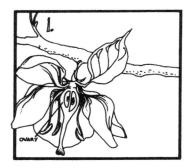   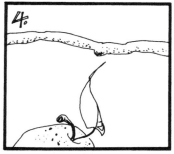

Most apple blossoms or flowers require cross-pollination for fertilization, unlike the daffodil that you examined earlier this month. If you have apple tree blossoms in your area and can examine a flower, look at its structure and parts. Draw a picture of what you see, including the inside parts. Draw your picture in the apple provided on the next page.

Do some research on apples and apple trees in books or on the Internet; then complete the apple tree crossword puzzle. Visit www.best apples.com/kids/color.html for more information. After completing the puzzle, you may want to try the delicious recipe for apple muffins that is given on the next page.

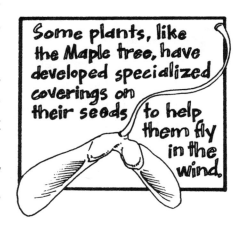

218

Caraway Apple Muffins

¼ cup butter	1 cup peeled and diced apples
⅓ cup sugar	1 cup milk
1 egg	sugar and cinnamon
2½ cups cake flour	muffin tins
½ tsp. salt	paper muffin cup liners
4 tsp. baking powder	
2 tsp. caraway seeds	*Yield:* 12 muffins

1. In a large bowl, beat the butter, sugar, and egg until the mixture is light and fluffy.

2. In another bowl, sift the cake flour, salt, and baking powder. Add and stir in the caraway seeds.

3. Add the dry mixture to the beaten egg mixture.

4. Add the milk and apple and mix well.

5. Place a cup liner in each opening in the muffin tin, and fill each one ⅔ full. Sprinkle with sugar and cinnamon.

6. Bake for 30 minutes at 375°F.

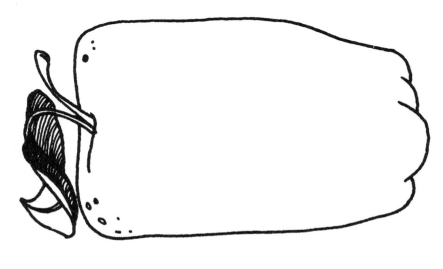

Note: This recipe is reproduced with the permission of Adelma Simmons, author of *The Book of Valentine Remembrances*, Caprilands Herb Farm, Coventry, Connecticut.

APPLE TREE CROSSWORD PUZZLE

Across

1. Because I'm an apple tree, I must rest in some parts of the country. I generally rest in the winter. When I'm resting, I'm _____.

4. I'm the last name of a legendary man who planted apple seeds across the country. I'm Johnny _____.

8. This is the season when you plant me in the South _____.

9. I'm the part of the apple tree that is the most sensitive. I must be buried deep in the ground. I'm the _____.

Down

2. I'm the delicious fruit from this tree. I'm full of vitamins A and C. I'm an _____.

3. I'm the actual last name of the pioneer and nurseryman who gave lots of pioneers apple seeds to plant. Johnny Appleseed became my nickname, but my real name is John _____.

5. When bees carry pollen from my flowers to another tree, they help pollinate me. This process is called cross-_____.

6. This is the season when you plant me in the North _____.

7. I'm the name given to a tree that's not as tall as it can be. I'm a _____ apple tree.

10. If my apple seeds are not ready to eat, they will be white. If the apple is ripe, the seeds are _____.

You might want to look up each type of apple in the drawing so you can color them correctly.

Golden Delicious · Rose of Caldaro · Calvilla · Delicious · Granny Smith · Jonathan

Activity Sheet 7.5.

Can Plants Grow in Outer Space?

Can plants grow in outer space? Can seeds grow that have been in outer space? Can grass grow on the moon? Can trees grow on Uranus? What do you think?

Read and find out what plants need for survival. Find four things that are essential to growth and development of plants. What are they? List them on the back of this page.

Read about the "canals of Mars." When scientists first saw them, what did they think they were? Would this mean Mars would be more likely or less likely to support plant life?

Now read about the moon and the planet Uranus. Cite any facts that you can to support you belief and findings as to why or why not plants could grow on the moon or on Uranus. Write those facts in the two planets below.

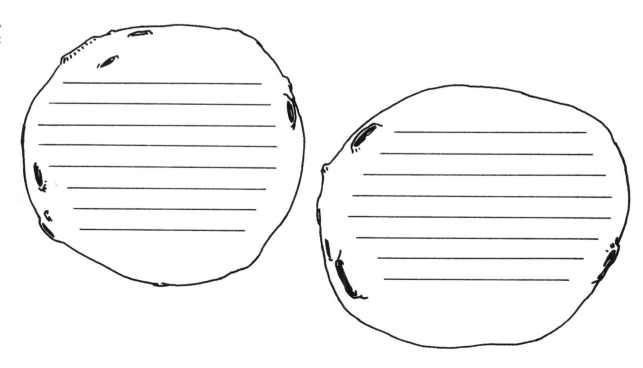

Activity Sheet 7.6.

What Is Light Refraction?

White light is composed of seven colors: red, orange, yellow, green, blue, indigo, and violet (remember them with this term, which uses the first letter of each color: ROY G. BIV). We can see these colors if we place a prism in the path of white light. This process of splitting up white light into a rainbow spectrum is called *refraction,* which is the bending of light. Because each color in the rainbow spectrum has a different wavelength, each color of white light bends at a different angle. The shortest wave (violet) bends the most and the longest wave (red) bends the least.

Materials

1 sheet of white paper

1 glass prism

sunlight

box of crayons

white paper

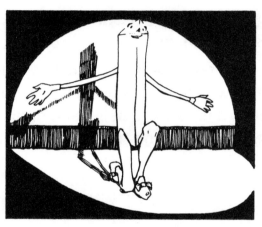

Procedure

1. Place the sheet of white paper under the prism.

2. Expose the prism to sunlight.

3. See how the white light from the sun separates into different colors on the white paper.

4. Use your crayons to draw the colors you see on the paper in order. How many colors are there? Which color is first? Use the space below for your colors.

What Is Light Refraction? *(Cont'd.)*

Conclusions

1. What color is bent the least?

2. True or false? The solar spectrum of color that you see here and in the rainbow is caused by the refraction or bending of the wavelengths of light. White light is a mixture of all these visible colors.

3. True or false? The longest wavelength of light we see is red and is bent the least.

4. True or false? The shortest wavelength of light we see is violet and is bent the most.

5. We can conclude that light passes through the air, into the _____ and back into the _____. This is called *refraction of light*.

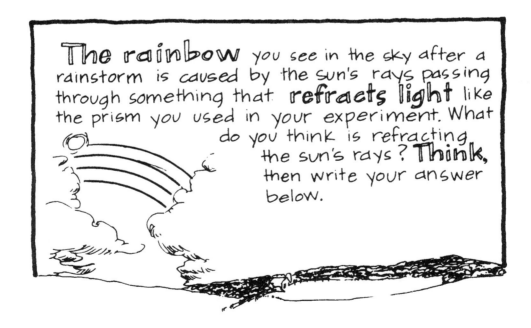

The rainbow you see in the sky after a rainstorm is caused by the sun's rays passing through something that **refracts light** like the prism you used in your experiment. What do you think is refracting the sun's rays? **Think,** then write your answer below.

Name _____   Date _____

St. Patrick's Day and the Shamrock

Before completing this puzzle, practice your researching skills by visiting Web sites to find the answers to these St. Patrick's Day and shamrock clues. Here are two sites you can visit: www.wikipedia.org/wiki/Legume and www.fi.edu/fellows/fellow7/mar99.

St. Patrick's Day and the Shamrock *(Cont'd.)*

Across

2. I'm a deep-rooted legume that grows in the ground. I'm used for hay and enjoyed by many animals. I'm an important part of the food chain. I'm _____.

3. When an object reflects green light wavelengths and absorbs other colors, I'm the color you see. I'm the color of chlorophyll, which is manufactured by plant cells. I'm _____.

5. I'm the legume that is worn on lapels on March 17. I'm also the national flower of Ireland. I'm a _____.

8. I'm the patron saint of Ireland. I'm _____.

Down

1. We're the legumes that grow erect or climb. We're rich in protein. We're _____.

4. We're the group of dicotyledons (plants with two seed leaves) whose fruit are used for food. Examples are beans, peas, clover, and soybeans. We're

    _____.

6. I'm a legume, and people search for four leaflets on me. I'm found covering the ground. I'm _____.

7. We're the reptiles that legend says St. Patrick drove into the sea off Ireland. We're _____.

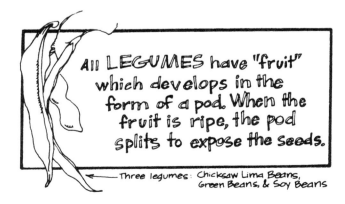

All LEGUMES have "fruit" which develops in the form of a pod. When the fruit is ripe, the pod splits to expose the seeds.

Three legumes: Chicksaw Lima Beans, Green Beans, & Soy Beans

Activity Sheet 7.8.

An Equinox "Egg-Speriment"

According to some, this equinox egg-speriment will work only on the day of the vernal equinox. What does the word *equinox* mean? Write its definition here:

_____

    Which one of the following illustrations shows the position of Earth and the sun at the time of the vernal equinox? Circle the correct Earth in its position around the sun.

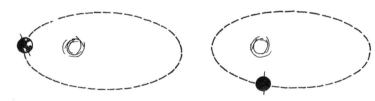

226

An Equinox "Egg-Speriment" *(Cont'd.)*

What time and day will the vernal equinox occur this year? Find out and write the time and day here:

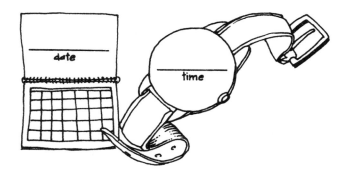

On that day and at that time, try to balance an egg on its end! Try both ends. Why do you think this egg might be balanced at this time and on this particular day? Explain your reasons on the back of this paper. On what other day of the year (besides the vernal equinox) might this occur? Why?

Caution: Everyone should wash hands after handling raw eggs.

An Equinox "Egg-Speriment" *(Cont'd.)*

Some scientists think this experiment can be performed on any day of the year and at any time. What do you think? Now that you've tried it on the vernal equinox, try it again on another day and time to see if it works as well.

After you have finished the "egg-speriment" with the eggs, you may want to make eggshell planters for the spring season. Boil as many eggs as you want planters and then carefully shell them; the eggshells can then be used as mini-planters for small seeds. (Use the hard-boiled eggs in a delicious egg salad!) Keep the last part of the shell intact so your planter will hold the seeds.

The outside of the eggshells can be decorated with acrylic paints. Then set the eggs in a cardboard holder, made by using tape or glue to make a loop out of a cardboard strip of paper about two inches wide and long enough to support your egg.

Your seedlings will probably have to be replanted if you want them to mature into fully grown plants.

Optional

Cut a small piece of sponge and put it in the bottom of the eggshell. Plant seeds on top of the sponge and water. Watch as the seed sprouts and the plant grows.

Activity Sheet 7.9.

Who's Who in the Food Chain?

Below are names of consumers and producers of a food chain. Which is the producer (the one on the bottom of the food chain)? After selecting the producer, write its name on the bottom line. Then list the consumers in the correct order in the food chain.

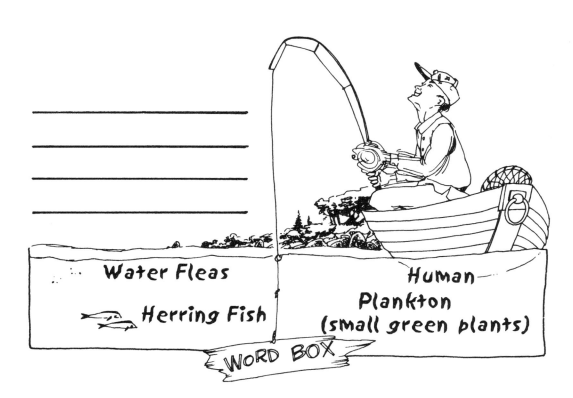

_____

_____

_____

_____

Water Fleas

Herring Fish

Human

Plankton
(small green plants)

WORD BOX

Vocabulary

producers

consumers

Who's Who in the Food Chain? *(Cont'd.)*

To understand how a food chain works, let's examine the plankton and small microscopic animals found in a drop of pond water.

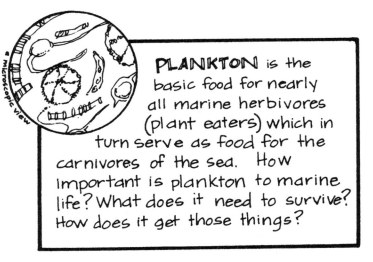

a microscopic view

PLANKTON is the basic food for nearly all marine herbivores (plant eaters) which in turn serve as food for the carnivores of the sea. How important is plankton to marine life? What does it need to survive? How does it get those things?

Materials

pond water containing a live specimen of freshwater *Crustacea* (or living invertebrate culture; see Appendix 2 for ordering information)

depressed microscopic slides and slide covers

microscope

eyedropper

Who's Who in the Food Chain? *(Cont'd.)*

Procedure

1. Place a drop of pond water or live culture onto the slide, which has been placed in position on the stage of the microscope.

2. Carefully place the slide cover on top of the depression.

3. Adjust the microscope to focus, and view the plankton and small crustaceans.

4. Draw a sketch of your observations in the circles below.

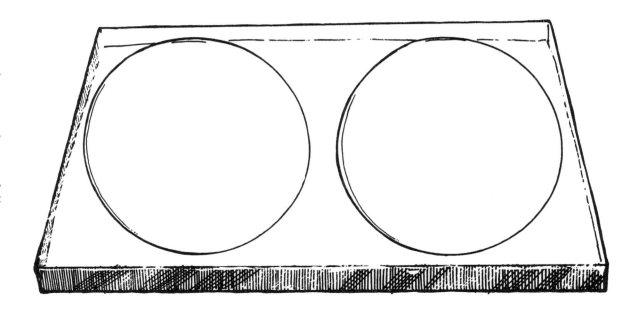

Conclusions

1. Can you identify or name any living invertebrates you saw?

2. What role do these small plants and animals play in the food chain?

231

Happy Birthday!

We recognize many famous people in science on their birthdays. On the cake below, write the name of a scientist of your choice and his or her birthday. Then describe in your own words why this person was important.

Why was this person important? _____

_____

_____

_____

MARCH

1 Find out about the flower of the month of March. Look at its parts. Observe and learn about trees in honor of Yellowstone National Park's birthday today, established in 1872.

2 Another famous national park was established today—Mount Rainier in 1899. Activity Sheet 7.2 will help you learn about Yellowstone and Mount Rainier National Parks.

3 Happy birthday, Florida! Activity Sheet 7.3 will help you find out more.

4 Happy birthday, Vermont! Why is the cow a symbol of this state? Read and find out! Do Activity Sheet 7.3 if you haven't done so already. Eat some pancakes with maple syrup!

5

6

MARCH

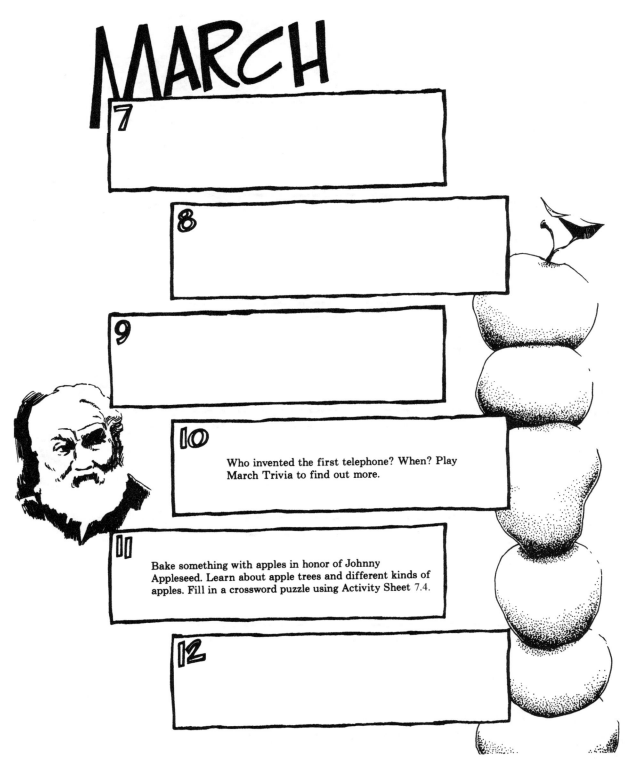

7

8

9

10 Who invented the first telephone? When? Play March Trivia to find out more.

11 Bake something with apples in honor of Johnny Appleseed. Learn about apple trees and different kinds of apples. Fill in a crossword puzzle using Activity Sheet 7.4.

12

MARCH

13 What is standard time? It was adopted today in 1884. Learn about the planet Uranus, discovered by Sir William Herschel in 1781. Do plants grow in outer space? See Activity Sheet 7.5.

14 Learn about light, rainbows, wavelengths, and prisms. Who was Albert Einstein? Why do we recognize him today? See Activity Sheet 7.6.

15

16

17 Find out about shamrocks. Celebrate St. Patrick's Day by doing Activity Sheet 7.7.

18 Play March Trivia to learn the name of the first human to walk in space.

MARCH

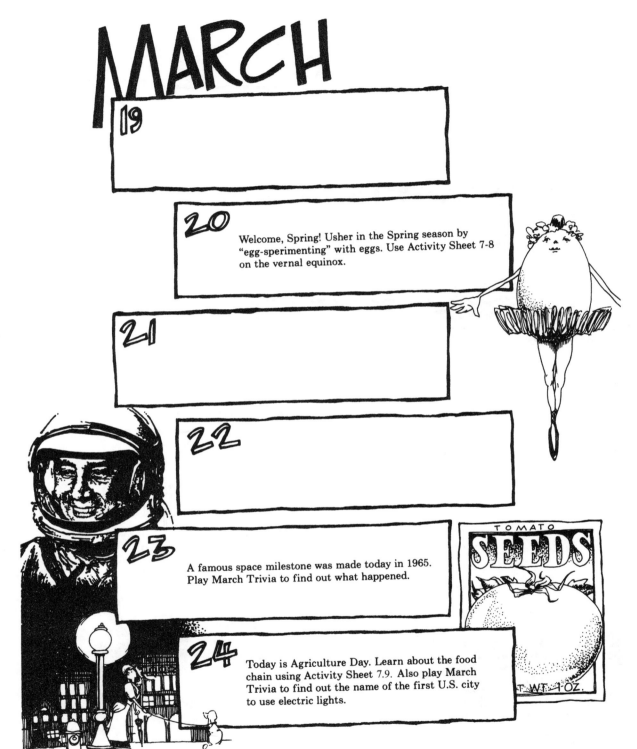

19

20 Welcome, Spring! Usher in the Spring season by "egg-sperimenting" with eggs. Use Activity Sheet 7-8 on the vernal equinox.

21

22

23 A famous space milestone was made today in 1965. Play March Trivia to find out what happened.

24 Today is Agriculture Day. Learn about the food chain using Activity Sheet 7.9. Also play March Trivia to find out the name of the first U.S. city to use electric lights.

TOMATO
SEEDS

T WT. 1 OZ.

236

MARCH

25 Learn about plant cells today. Happy Birthday, Max Johann Sigismund Schulze.

26 Learn about how to prevent infectious diseases, like tuberculosis, thanks to scientists like Robert Koch, Nobel Prize winner.

27 Happy Birthday to Karl Wilhelm von Nageli. Find out about single and multicellular plants.

28

29

30/31 Happy Birthday, Victor Mills. Learn about how this scientist improved some of the foods you've eaten.

April

April is Earth Month—an exciting month to teach science with a focus on the environment.

The idea for Earth Month is derived from the first official Earth Day held on April 22, 1970. Since then, millions of people have become more conscientious and concerned about protecting and developing Earth's finite resources.

As educators, we must teach children about everyone's responsibility to the planet. Learning how to care for, respect, develop, and protect our resources—flora, fauna, air, land, water—is essential to the survival of all life on Earth.

Some April Dates to Remember and Background Information for the Activities

Activity sheets are provided for starred dates only. It is your decision whether to give the students facts on each entry. And for the trivia game referred to, go to Appendix 5.

* *First Sunday in April.* This is the time to change to daylight saving time. See Activity Sheet 8.1.

1* *First weather satellite launched (1960).* The first weather satellite was launched from Cape Canaveral, Florida, on this date in 1960. Thirty years later (see April 24 entry), the Hubble space telescope was launched from the space shuttle *Discovery*. (See Activity Sheet 8.2.) The Hubble travels in an orbit around the planet. Because it's located outside Earth's atmosphere, this telescope is able to take optical photographs of faint and distant objects. Since its launch in 1990, the Hubble has become one of the most important telescopes in the history of astronomy, adding greatly to our understanding of the universe. For the latest news on the Hubble space telescope and to see various photos the telescope has sent back from space, visit the NASA Web site at www.hubble.nasa.gov/index.php.

2 *Florida Day.* Celebrate the landing of Juan Ponce de Leon in Florida in 1513.

6 *Discovery of the North Pole (1909).* The first successful expedition to the North Pole was led by Robert Peary.

7* *World Health Organization founded (1948).* Discuss the benefits of this month. Important points to keep in mind are recycling (see Activity Sheet 8.3) and preserving our national parks (see Activity Sheet 8.4). The World Health Organization (WHO), located in Geneva, Switzerland, is an agency of the United Nations that focuses on coordinating international public health issues. WHO's major focus is combating disease and promoting the health around the world. This month you can discuss the importance and benefits of WHO. For more information on WHO, have your students visit the official site at www.who.int/en.

8* *Chemical leak disaster at Bhopal (1984).* The Indian government filed a lawsuit against Union Carbide Corporation for a toxic chemical leak at Bhopal that caused thousands of casualties. This was an extreme form of air pollution, but other things in the air can also harm people, animals, and plants. Discuss clean air with your students, and use Activity Sheet 8.5 to learn more.

9* *Lower Mississippi River claimed for France (1682).* This now-famous river area was discovered by explorer Robert de La Salle and named "Louisiana" after the French king. Discuss water pollution, including its causes and effects on animals and plants in the water, with your students, and have them complete Activity Sheet 8.6. (Also see the April 17 entry.)

10* *Arbor Day originally observed.* Arbor Day was first observed in Nebraska in 1872. You may have your students do Activity Sheet 8.7 either today or on the last Friday in April, when Arbor Day is now observed.

12 *Polio vaccine declared safe (1955).* Jonas Salk, a U.S. physician and bacteriologist, developed a vaccine to prevent poliomyelitis.

13 *Thomas Jefferson born (1743).* Jefferson, one of the most important participants in the founding of the United States and its third president, owned a large plantation called Monticello in Virginia and was famous for many fine inventions. Read about Jefferson to see which of his inventions you find interesting, and create a trivia question-and-answer game card.

14 *Demonstration of first commercial videotape recorder (1956).* This historic first was demonstrated by the Ampex Corporation.

17* *New York Harbor discovered (1524).* This discovery was made by Giovanni da Verrazano. If you haven't already given your students Activity Sheet 8.6, you might do so today.

19* *Birthday of Richard Pough (1904).* Pough, an American ecologist, was the founder of the Nature Conservatory, the nation's largest environmental organization. He also helped develop the World Wildlife Fund and was especially fascinated by hawks. Pough was acutely aware of the dangers of DDT and warned it could make animals extinct. He also is the author of the *Audubon Bird Guide.*

Have students research Pough and complete a biographical sketch on him using the form in Appendix 6. They can also read about hawks in the *Audubon Bird Guide* or have students research both the Nature Conservatory and the World Wildlife Fund using Activity Sheet 8.8. Here they will complete a Venn diagram comparing the two organizations and their purposes: how they are similar and different.

21* *Birthday of John Muir (1838).* Muir was a naturalist and conservationist who established the Sequoia and Yosemite National Parks in California. Activity Sheet 8.4 helps students understand the importance of forest and wildlife conservation in our national parks. You may also want them to research the Sequoia and Yosemite parks and find out about each. John Muir is considered the father of the national park system. Use the Science Report Plaque in Appendix 6.

24 *Hubble space telescope launched by crew of* Discovery *(1990).*

25 *St. Lawrence Seaway opened to shipping (1959).*

26* *Nuclear accident in Chernobyl (1986).* The Chernobyl accident occurred on April 26, 1986, at the Chernobyl nuclear power plant in Ukraine (which at the time was a part of the Soviet Union). This is regarded as the worst accident in the history of nuclear power. Since the Chernobyl nuclear power plant did not have a containment building, a plume of radioactive fallout spread far and wide across the continent. This resulted in the relocation of approximately two hundred thousand people. The process of decontamination was and continues to be massive and costly, and countless numbers of people continue to suffer the effects of radioactive exposure. Visit www.chernobyl.co.uk for more information about this devastating event. See Activity Sheet 8.5.

26* *John James Audubon born (1785).* This famous naturalist was also an excellent artist. He painted many species of birds, some of which are now endangered. An animal, or species of animals, becomes endangered when its population becomes so small that it is at risk of becoming extinct, or ceases to exist. A famous example of an extinct animal is the dodo bird. In 1973, the Endangered Species Act was passed in the United States to help protect critical animals from becoming extinct. This was one of many laws passed in the 1970s in an attempt to stop or reverse the degradation of the environment. This act not only protected animals, but also protected whole ecosystems that those animals needed in order to survive. See Activity Sheet 8.9.

30 *Louisiana was admitted to the Union (1812). Hawaii became a territory of the United States. (1900).* Hawaii did not become a state until 1959.

Activity Sheet 8.1.

Let's Save Lots of Watts!

The first Sunday in April is the official beginning of daylight saving time. On this day, most states move their clocks ahead one hour: "Spring ahead, fall back." Daylight saving time lasts until the last Sunday in October, when the clocks are set back one hour.

This later hour of sunlight helps save energy because we are able to use the sun's energy for one hour longer at the end of the day.

How can you save energy at home and school? When your parents go shopping for lightbulbs, help them select wisely. Look at the package for information about the lightbulb. Higher wattage does not mean a brighter bulb. Brightness is measured in lumens, not in watts. Look for the most lumens with the fewest watts. This kind of bulb is more *energy-efficient*. Watts measure the bulb's use of energy.

Visit the U.S. Department of Energy Web site for the Bright Idea facts on energy-efficient lightbulbs: www.ftc.gov/bcp/conline/pubs/products/ffclight.htm.

Go on an energy-saving hunt at home. Use the checklist and help save energy. Be wise and save lots of watts!

> **Caution:** Check with your parent before beginning this hunt. You might have an adult with you to do this evaluation.

Vocabulary
lumens

watts

energy-efficient

Let's Save Lots of Watts! *(Cont'd.)*

❑ Look at where your lamps and lighting fixtures are in your house. Should some of them be rearranged for improvements in lighting? Do you have good lighting where you read?

❑ Take time to find out about different types of lightbulbs available. Some new bulbs are designed to last longer and save money. Some are more efficient than others. Find at least two types of lightbulbs that you have never used in your home, and explain the bulbs' special features on the back of this paper.

❑ Do you use timers or dimmers in your home? What do they do? How do they help save energy?

❑ Keep your lampshades and bulbs clean. Dust impedes the brightness of light. Why?

❑ Look outside your house, and find out about types of bulbs for outdoors. There are special bulbs for lighting patios, yards, and garages that are different from indoor bulbs. They can also save money and energy. Learn about one outdoor bulb, and describe it below.

Let's Save Lots of Watts! *(Cont'd.)*

PICK THE MOST
ENERGY-EFFICIENT BULB

Bulb A : 1,500 lumens
100 watts

Bulb B : 1,700 lumens
75 watts

Bulb C : 1,400 lumens
120 watts

ANSWER: _____

Activity Sheet 8.2.

The Hubble

On April 24, 1990, the $1.5 billion Hubble space tele-
scope was launched with the space shuttle **Discovery.**
Since then it has continued to orbit Earth and take
optical photographs of distant and faint objects in
space. The photos that it sends back to Earth are mar-
velous. Visit the Hubble Web site for a gallery of
images at www.hubble.nasa.gov/index.php.

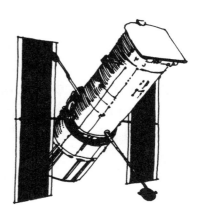

Complete the chart below with the latest information you can find on the Internet about the Hubble.
What are the latest photographs that have been sent
back to Earth? Has anything been discovered recently?

Date	Event	Source of Information	Results of Information Discovered

Want to Know More?

- Read about the U.S. astronomer Edwin Hubble.
- What are cosmic X-rays? Gamma rays?
- What is a galaxy? A supernova? A quasar?

What Can We Recycle?

What does *recycling* mean? Why is it important to recycle anything? How does recycling help our environment? Discuss these questions with your family and classmates. Before you throw anything away, always check for a symbol on your glass, plastic, and tin containers to see if they're recyclable. Visit the following site for tips on how you can reduce, reuse, and recycle in your daily life and for a picture of the international recycling symbol: www.bogfrog.com/fftips3rs.htm.

Write the definition of *biodegradable, nonbiodegradable, returnables, recyclable,* and *reusable* on the back of this page.

Activity Sheet 8.4.

How Can We Help Our National Parks?

Last month, you learned about Yellowstone National Park's anniversary on March 1, 1872. This park covers 2.2 million acres and is the home to many animals, trees, and plants. It was America's first national park.

What are some ways that people can help parks or natural wilderness areas such as Yellowstone keep their balance of nature? *Conservation* is a word that means careful use and preservation of natural resources: plants, animals, water, air, and soil.

Look at the two charts labeled "Forest conservation" and "Wildlife conservation." Then read and think about the statements on the next page. Write the number of the statements that belong in either—or both—of the two charts. (Some statements apply to both.)

For more information, visit the National Park Service Web site at www.nps.gov.

Vocabulary
conservation

Forest conservation

Wildlife conservation

249

How Can We Help Our National Parks? *(Cont'd.)*

Statements

1. Don't cut down too many trees. Recycle paper instead. Every ton of recycled paper saves seventeen trees.

2. Check trees for harmful insects. Many insects kill trees by destroying leaves and wood.

3. People should hunt for certain animals only during open hunting seasons and only in designated areas, according to law.

4. People must observe the limits set on hunting. The number of fish, birds, deer, and other game hunted should be restricted.

5. Plant seedlings to help forests and trees grow.

6. Any endangered species should not be hunted at any time. Help these animals grow, survive, and have future generations.

7. Be very careful in the parks when using fire. Fire can destroy both animals and trees.

Activity Sheet 8.5.

How Important Is Clean Air?

Do you think it is important to keep the air clean? How can this be done? How does the air become polluted? Does this affect plants and animals? How?

What is the Clean Air Act? How does it help keep air clean? What can be done to protect and purify our air?

pH is a measure of acidity or alkalinity in a solution. It represents and measures the concentration of hydrogen ions in water. Acids are usually sour-tasting substances, like lemon juice, and alkalis (bases) are substances that are bitter tasting, like baking soda. pH is measured on a scale of 0 to 14, with 7 being neutral. Solutions that measure from 0 to 6 are acids, and solutions that measure from 8 to 14 are bases. pH is most commonly measured with a pH meter, which is an electronic device with a probe.

It's important that the pH levels in the air, water, and soil are at a safe level. Because we live in a balanced ecosystem, the pH level of air affects the level of pH in water and in the soil. For example, air pollution from cars creates an acidic pH in the air atmosphere. When it rains, the acidic pH from the air creates acid rain, which is then absorbed in the soil.

Your teacher will perform the following investigations to show the importance and function of respiration in animals and plants and the carbon dioxide/ oxygen cycle of gas exchange. For more information on pH levels and its effects on the environment, visit bcn.boulder.co.us/basin/data/COBWQ/info/pH.html.

Vocabulary
pollution
pH

Warning: This is a teacher demonstration only.

How Important Is Clean Air? *(Cont'd.)*

Materials

limewater

glass jar

2 straws

Procedure

1. Pour the limewater into a glass jar.
2. Using the straw, carefully blow into the limewater. **Be sure to exhale, not inhale!**
3. Observe what happens to the color of the limewater.

Conclusions

1. What does the color or change in the limewater indicate?
2. What gas was bubbled into the limewater?

Additional Activity

This activity demonstrates the carbon dioxide–oxygen exchange cycle.

Materials

6 test tubes with screw tops (culture tubes) or foil on top

tap water

bromthymol blue (a pH indicator available at a pet store)

straw

baking soda (optional)

4 sprigs of elodea (available at pet stores)

4 live snails

2 test tube holders

light

252

How Important Is Clean Air? *(Cont'd.)*

Procedure

1. Fill each of the six test tubes with the same amount of tap water.

2. Take the pH of each tube by adding small amounts of bromthymol blue according to the directions on the bottle. The water's color will indicate its acidity, varying from yellow (slightly acid) to green, blue-green, and deep blue.

3. Now use a straw and blow into the blue water. **Be sure to exhale, not inhale!** The carbon dioxide will dissolve and lower the pH you just established, changing the color from blue to yellow. Adding a little baking soda or more bromthymol blue will adjust the pH back to basic blue.

4. Once the pH is adjusted to blue, set up three test tubes: one with a snail alone, one with a sprig of elodea alone, and one with a snail and elodea together. Repeat with three other test tubes. Place three test tubes in one holder and the other three test tubes in the second holder.

5. Set one holder with three tubes under a light, and leave it for several days. Set the other holder with three tubes in a dark place (such as a closet), and leave it for several days. Observe each daily, and watch the color of the water. After three days, test the water in each test tube for pH levels, and record your findings on the back of this paper. Be sure to let the snails go in their natural habitat once the experiment is over.

Conclusions

1. What did the test tubes show about the level of acidity in the tubes with the snail alone? With the elodea alone? With the snail and elodea together?

2. How did light affect the experiment? How is this like photosynthesis?

How Important Is Clean Air? *(Cont'd.)*

Natural Air Purifiers

When you inhale, you breathe in oxygen and exhale carbon dioxide. Your teacher's simple experiment using limewater demonstrated this respiration process.

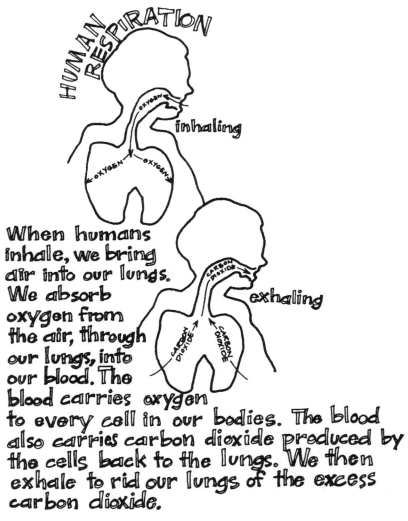

HUMAN RESPIRATION

inhaling

exhaling

When humans inhale, we bring air into our lungs. We absorb oxygen from the air, through our lungs, into our blood. The blood carries oxygen to every cell in our bodies. The blood also carries carbon dioxide produced by the cells back to the lungs. We then exhale to rid our lungs of the excess carbon dioxide.

Plants breathe in carbon dioxide and exhale oxygen. They are important to the balance of nature. Some air purifiers are electrical devices that help remove impurities from the air. You may want to examine one if you have one at home or in the classroom.

How Important Is Clean Air? *(Cont'd.)*

PLANT RESPIRATION

CARBON DIOXIDE

OXYGEN

Plant respiration takes place in STOMATA— small holes in the undersides of leaves. Carbon dioxide enters the leaves through these holes, while the oxygen, produced by the plant during respiration, leaves through these stomata.

What are natural, organic air purifiers? If you guessed "green plants," you are right! It has been estimated that a 1,500-square-foot home or office can benefit by the contributions of fifteen green foliage plants. The plants absorb certain toxic gases in the air and improve the air by releasing oxygen. Some of the toxic gases that plants remove are carbon monoxide, formaldehyde, benzene, and carbon dioxide. Purifying the air makes breathing easier for humans!

255

Activity Sheet 8.6.

Making Our Water Safe

Do you live near any major rivers or oceans? What is "polluted water"? How does water become polluted? How does pollution affect plants and animals?

Are there any laws in your region or state to protect the water? What is the Clean Water Act? What can you do to protect and improve the water in the rivers and oceans? Find out more about water pollution at the library or on the Internet. Two good reference sites to visit for the Clean Water Act and for water pollution are enviro.blr.com/topic.cfm/topic/442/state/155 and nature.org.

In the picture below, find and circle the marine animals that could be adversely affected by polluted water. Select one of these animals, and read about it in your library or online. Write a few facts about the animal on the back of this paper. Then do the water investigation on the next page.

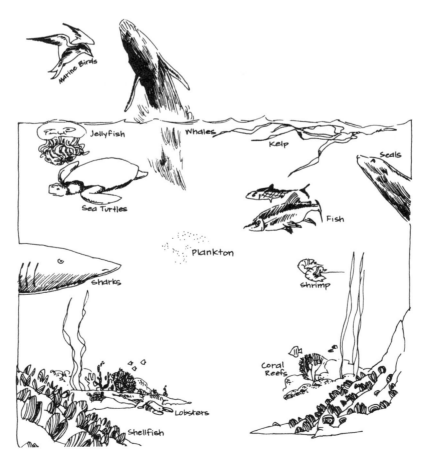

Making Our Water Safe *(Cont'd.)*

Investigating Water

Have you ever set up an aquarium for fish? Did the water become cloudy? Do you know why?

Water contains the elements *hydrogen* and *oxygen*. The formula H_2O means that there is one part oxygen to two parts hydrogen. Fish use the oxygen from the atmosphere, which is dissolved in the water. The problem is that other gases, wastes, and solids sometimes pollute or contaminate the water that fish and other marine life need to survive.

Fish do not have lungs. Instead, they use their gills to filter the gases and breathe oxygen and then eliminate carbon dioxide. Water can be conditioned to improve its nature. Conditioning helps remove toxic chlorine gas. Here's how.

Materials

> 3 clean fish tanks of the same size
>
> fresh tap water
>
> 2 aerating stones
>
> aquarium plants

Procedure

1. Place the three tanks in three locations: two in direct sunlight and one in a shady spot.
2. Fill each fish tank with 1 gallon of fresh tap water.
3. Place an aerating stone in each of the two tanks in direct sun.
4. Place the plants in one of the two tanks with an aerating stone.
5. Leave the tanks undisturbed for one week.

Making Our Water Safe *(Cont'd.)*

Conclusions

1. Which tank's water is the first to be "conditioned" for fish? Why?
2. How did the stones help?
3. How did the plants help?

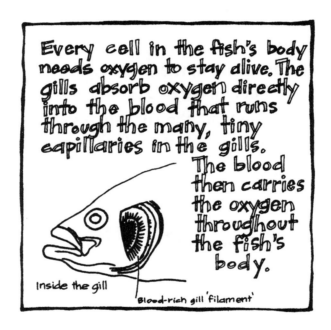

Every cell in the fish's body needs oxygen to stay alive. The gills absorb oxygen directly into the blood that runs through the many, tiny capillaries in the gills.

The blood then carries the oxygen throughout the fish's body.

Inside the gill

Blood-rich gill 'filament'

For Further Investigation

Find out about the Marine Mammal Protection Agency.

Activity Sheet 8.7.

Honor Arbor Day by Planting a Seedling

Most states celebrate Arbor Day on the last Friday of April. Arbor Day was first observed in Nebraska on April 10, 1872. Since then, many seedlings have been planted that help forests grow and help restore the balance of trees, many of which are cut unnecessarily. Here's a way for you to help with this effort.

1. Select a Seedling

Name of seedling you will plant:

_____

Conditions needed for growth (list any facts you know about the parent tree with regard to size, soil, light, water requirements, and so on):

_____

_____

2. Select a Site

Is your seedling native to your area? Why is this important?

_____

_____

Where will you plant the seedling? Consider competition with other plants, trees, and space:

_____

_____

Honor Arbor Day by Planting a Seedling *(Cont'd.)*

Make a signpost for your seedling. You may want to provide information such as the name of the tree—its Latin name, its common name, or both. Write here what it will say:

_____

_____

3. Plant Your Seedling

If possible, analyze the soil prior to planting. Use either a soil-testing kit or send the soil to a nearby extension office for analysis. Does your soil need nutrients or fertilizer? Do you need to use compost? What size and depth of hole must be made for your seedling? Who will dig the hole? What tools will that person need?

   After planning and answering these questions, you are ready to plant the seedling. Don't forget to tend to it after it is planted. Water the seedling, but be sure not to overwater.

4. Results

Use a camera to photograph your seedling (especially on Arbor Day) throughout the rest of the school year. Measure its growth. When you return to school in the fall, measure the seedling's growth again and note the results.

Activity Sheet 8.8.

Comparing Environmental Organizations

Two large environmental groups that you may have heard of are the World Wildlife Fund and the Nature Conservancy. Learn more about them from their Web sites: www.worldwildlife.org and www.nature.org.

After browsing these two sites, complete the diagram below to compare and contrast the two organizations. In the large circle on the left, write information about the World Wildlife Fund. In the large circle on the right, write information about the Nature Conservancy. In the overlapping circle area in the middle, write information that applies to both organizations.

Who was Richard Pough, and what was his relationship to these two groups? Write a mini-report or biographical sketch using the forms provided.

Activity Sheet 8.9.

Endangered Species

What does *endangered species* mean? Look at the picture below. It shows ten North American animals and two plants that are endangered. Read about each animal and plant, and write a few facts about them on the back of this paper. Then match the animals and plants to their names by writing the correct numeral next to each name. How can we help these animals and plants from becoming extinct? What does *extinct* mean? Does *endangered* mean the same as *extinct*?

   Name one animal that has become extinct. Draw and write about it on the next page. Find out about the Endangered Species Act. What is it? For a federal list of endangered wildlife and plants, visit the U.S. Fish and Wildlife Service Web site at www.fws.gov/endangered/wildlife.html.

_____ Schaus swallowtail butterfly   _____ red-cockaded woodpecker

_____ American crocodile   _____ eastern indigo snake

_____ gila trout   _____ northern aplomado falcon

_____ black-capped vireo   _____ Florida panther

_____ running buffalo clover   _____ whooping crane

_____ Aleutian Canada goose   _____ small whorled pogonia

Extinct Animal's Name: _____
Describe its environment _____
_____

Drawing of Extinct Animal

Remember to include the extinct animal's environment in your drawing.

How did this animal become extinct?
(Write your answer below.)

_____
_____
_____
_____
_____

APRIL

1 What's the weather like today? The first weather satellite was launched in 1960 from Cape Canaveral, Florida. Tomorrow is Florida Day. Why?

2 What famous navigator landed in Florida on this day in 1513? Play April Trivia to find out.

3

4

5

6 Think about the North Pole on this day to commemorate the first expedition there led by Robert Peary in 1909. Write a science mini-report on the North Pole.

APRIL

7 What is the World Health Organization? How are needy people helped in other countries? How are people educated about nutrition and good health habits? Brainstorm with your classmates to list ways.

8 A tragic chemical leak occurred in Bhopal, India, in 1984. Learn about clean air, and the oxygen–carbon dioxide cycle in plants and animals. Use Activity Sheet 8.5.

9 The Mississippi River was discovered by European explorers today in 1682. How can we keep our rivers clean? Brainstorm with your classmates to list ways. Learn about clean water for aquatic animals and find out how to remove toxic gases. Use Activity Sheet 8.6.

10 Nebraska celebrated the first Arbor Day in 1872. Activity Sheet 8.7 can be done today or on the last Friday in April. How do plants and trees help improve the quality of air? Plant a seedling.

11

12 What is the Salk vaccine? Are there different vaccines for polio available today? Talk to your school nurse or doctor to learn more.

Bhopal

INDIA

POLIO VACCINATIONS →

APRIL

13 Who was Thomas Jefferson? What did he invent? What did he write? Read about him and his many contributions. Write a biography sketch of him.

14 The first commercial videotape recorder was shown today in 1956. Nowadays, DVD players are the standard household equipment. Watch a science DVD or record your own science demonstration.

15

16

17 New York Harbor was discovered by European explorers today in 1524. Learn about clean water by doing Activity Sheet 8.6 (if you haven't already done the activity).

18

APRIL

19 Happy Birthday, Richard Pough, founder of the Nature Conservatory. Pough helped develop the World Wildlife Fund. He also wrote what book?

20

21 Happy Birthday, John Muir, father of our national parks. Celebrate with Activity Sheet 8.4.

22

23

24

APRIL

CANADA

USA

25 St. Lawrence Seaway opened for shipping today in 1959. Look at a map and locate the seaway.

26 Happy Birthday, John James Audubon. He was born today in 1785. Do Activity Sheet 8.9. Write a biographical sketch of him.

27

28

29

Mississippi River

☆ Baton Rouge

New Orleans

30 What happened to Louisiana and Hawaii today? Find out.

May–June

The months of May and June are combined to present a science potpourri of activities that review and culminate the concepts and activities presented all year.

Since September, students have learned about famous people and their contributions, inventions, and discoveries. They have learned about space and space travel, matter, plants, animals, food chains, ecology, pollution, conservation, and energy. Your students have also learned about caring for the planet Earth and about personal health and nutrition.

Students have been encouraged to think scientifically, to interpret data and form conclusions, to observe, and to classify. They have been encouraged to inquire and ask questions as they accumulated data through investigation, reading, and discussion.

By recognizing the dates and events that have made a difference in our world's progress, they too may be challenged to discover, invent, and create!

Some May and June Dates to Remember and Background Information for the Activities

Activity sheets are provided for starred dates only. It is your decision whether to give the students facts on each entry. And for the trivia game referred to, go to Appendix 5.

May

1* *May Day.* Celebrate the first of May by planning or participating in a science fair. See Activity Sheet 9.1. Here students will have the opportunity to follow the scientific method by observing, formulating hypotheses, experimenting, and drawing conclusions. Be sure to review the scientific method with students before they begin the activity.

The scientific method is the process that scientists go through to create an accurate representation of the world:

1. *Observation:* Watch, study, and observe some particular aspect of or phenomenon in the world.
2. *Hypothesis:* Based on what you've observed, create a tentative description of what you observed, known as a *hypothesis.*
3. *Prediction:* Use your hypothesis to make predictions of what will happen in the future.
4. *Experiment:* Test your hypothesis with an experiment. Change your hypothesis to align with the results of your experiment.
5. *Conclusion:* Repeat steps 3 and 4 until there are no discrepancies between your hypothesis and observations. The result is your conclusion.

4* *Invisible ink first used in diplomatic correspondence (1776).* Students will enjoy writing messages using invisible ink. On this day in 1776, a member of the American colonies' Committee of Secret Correspondence went to France carrying a coded military statement written in invisible ink. Activity Sheet 9.2 will give students the opportunity to do the same, only they'll write science facts, not military secrets!

5 *First American in space (1961).* Alan B. Shepard Jr. was the astronaut of the first American manned space flight. His craft was the *Mercury-Redstone 3.* His flight lasted fifteen minutes.

8* *Coca-Cola invented (1886).* John Styth Pemberton, an Atlanta, Georgia, pharmacist, invented a syrup in his own backyard. This syrup was sold to a pharmacy and ultimately became the first Coca-Cola drink.

Have students read about the nutritional information on a bottle or can of cola and do Activity Sheet 9.3 to find out about caffeine and its effects. Visit the Coca-Cola Web site at www.cocacola.com.

9 *First airplane flown over the North Pole (1926).* The pilots of this historic flight were Richard Byrd and Floyd Bennett.

10 *First U.S. transcontinental railroad completed in Utah (1869).*

12* *Birthday of Florence Nightingale (1820).* The founder of modern nursing was born in England. Talk with your students about careers in medicine and nursing. Compare the professions today to those when Florence Nightingale was alive. See Activity Sheet 9.4.

14 *Smallpox vaccine discovered (1796).* This important discovery was made by Dr. Edward Jenner.

14* *First manned space station,* Skylab I, *launched (1973).* See Activity Sheet 9.5.

Third Week in May* *International Pickle Week.* Activity Sheet 9.6 is provided for fun and investigation.

20 *Charles Lindbergh flew from Long Island to Paris (1927).* He landed his famous airplane, the *Spirit of St. Louis,* outside Paris after crossing the Atlantic Ocean. The flight took him thirty-three and a half hours. See Activity Sheet 9.5.

20 *Amelia Earhart flew solo across the Atlantic Ocean (1932).* She was the first woman to fly solo across the Atlantic, from Newfoundland to Ireland. See Activity Sheet 9.5.

20 *Birthday of William Hewlett (1931).* William Redington Hewlett was an American electrical engineer who was a leader in the manufacture of computers and printers. In graduate school, Hewlett created an audio oscillator, circuitry that amplifies and delivers sounds, which he sold to Walt Disney Studios to use in making the movie *Fantasia.* When he was twenty-six years old, after graduating from Stanford, he partnered with David Packard, and the two formed the manufacturing business Hewlett-Packard, with an initial capital investment of $538.

Students may want to research Hewlett on the Internet and find out about the growth of his business today (www.hp.com). Hewlett died on January 12, 2001. The biographical report form in Appendix 6 can be used for this research.

June

3* *First American walked in space (1965).* Edward White was the first American to walk in space during the *Gemini-Titan 4* mission. See Activity Sheet 9.5.

4 *Henry Ford successfully tested his first car in Detroit (1896).*

12 *Cat gave birth to her 420th kitten (1952).* A cat named Dusty gave birth to her record-breaking kitten at the age of seventeen in Texas. Have students check the *Guinness Book of World Records* for details on this and other fascinating facts.

16 *First woman in space (1963).* Russian cosmonaut Valentina Tereshkova made forty-eight orbits around Earth aboard *Vostok 6.*

18* *First American woman in space (1983).* Sally Ride flew aboard the space shuttle *Challenger.* See Activity Sheet 9.5.

20–23* *Summer solstice.* Discuss the positions of Earth and the sun during the summer solstice. (See the following illustration.) Explain that Earth's axis is tilted at an angle of 23½ degrees to the sun and that it moves clockwise around the sun in an elliptical orbit. Give students Activity Sheet 9.7 to celebrate the arrival of summer. There are more hours of sunlight on the day of the summer solstice than on any other day of the year. The North Pole tilts toward the sun, and the South Pole is dark.

25 *Record high U.S. temperature for June (2006).* A U.S. record June high of 125°F was set in Death Valley, California. Summer had arrived! (The all-time record high for the U.S. was 134°F set in Greenland Ranch, California, on July 10, 1913.)

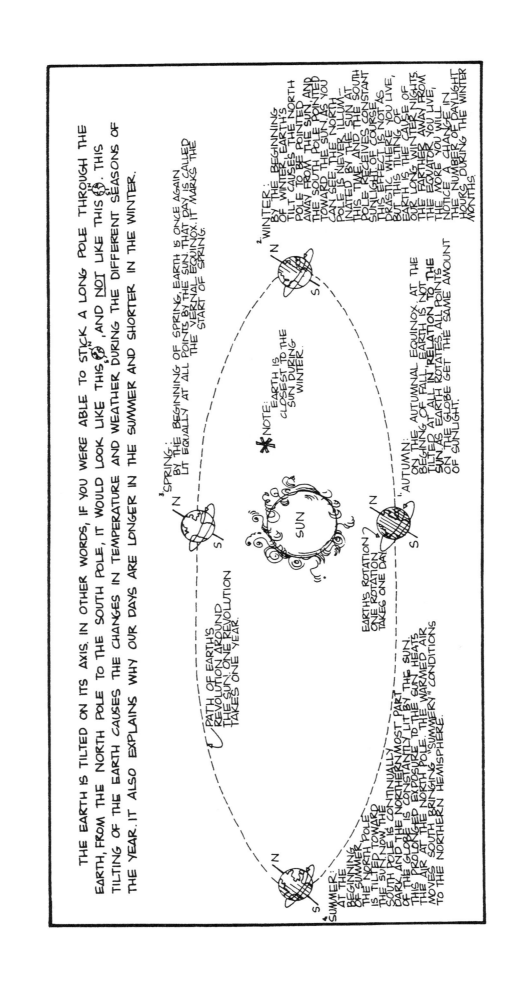

THE EARTH IS TILTED ON ITS AXIS. IN OTHER WORDS, IF YOU WERE ABLE TO STICK A LONG POLE THROUGH THE EARTH, FROM THE NORTH POLE TO THE SOUTH POLE, IT WOULD LOOK LIKE THIS, AND NOT LIKE THIS. THIS TILTING OF THE EARTH CAUSES THE CHANGES IN TEMPERATURE AND WEATHER DURING THE DIFFERENT SEASONS OF THE YEAR. IT ALSO EXPLAINS WHY OUR DAYS ARE LONGER IN THE SUMMER AND SHORTER IN THE WINTER.

SUN

PATH OF EARTH'S REVOLUTION AROUND THE SUN. ONE REVOLUTION TAKES ONE YEAR.

EARTHS ROTATION ONE ROTATION TAKES ONE DAY.

NOTE: EARTH IS CLOSEST TO THE SUN DURING WINTER.

2. WINTER: BY THE BEGINNING OF WINTER EARTH'S TILT CAUSES THE NORTH POLE TO BE POINTED AWAY FROM THE SUN AND THE SOUTH POLE POINTED TOWARD THE SUN. AS YOU CAN SEE THE NORTH POLE IS NEVER ILLUMINATED BY THE SUN AT THIS TIME. AND THE SOUTH POLE RECEIVES CONSTANT SUNLIGHT. OF COURSE THIS EFFECT IS NOT AS DRASTIC WHERE YOU LIVE, BUT THIS TILTING OF EARTH IS THE CAUSE OF OUR LONG WINTER NIGHTS. THE FARTHER AWAY FROM THE EQUATOR YOU LIVE, THE MORE YOU WILL NOTICE A CHANGE IN THE NUMBER OF DAYLIGHT HOURS DURING THE WINTER MONTHS.

3. SPRING: BY THE BEGINNING OF SPRING, EARTH IS ONCE AGAIN LIT EQUALLY AT ALL POINTS BY THE SUN. THAT DAY IS CALLED THE VERNAL EQUINOX. IT MARKS THE START OF SPRING.

1. AUTUMN: ON THE AUTUMNAL EQUINOX, AT THE BEGINNING OF FALL, EARTH IS NOT TILTED AT ALL IN RELATION TO THE SUN. AS EARTH ROTATES ALL POINTS ON THE GLOBE GET THE SAME AMOUNT OF SUNLIGHT.

4. SUMMER: AT THE BEGINNING OF SUMMER THE NORTH POLE IS TILTED TOWARD THE SUN. NOW THE SOUTH POLE IS CONTINUALLY DARK, AND THE NORTHERNMOST PART OF THE GLOBE IS CONSTANTLY LIT BY THE SUN. THIS PROLONGED EXPOSURE TO THE SUN HEATS THE AIR AT THE NORTH POLE. THE WARMED AIR MOVES SOUTH BRINGING SUMMERY CONDITIONS TO THE NORTHERN HEMISPHERE.

Name ____________________ Date ____________

Activity Sheet 9.1.

Proposal for a Science Fair Project

What will you make, invent, or demonstrate?

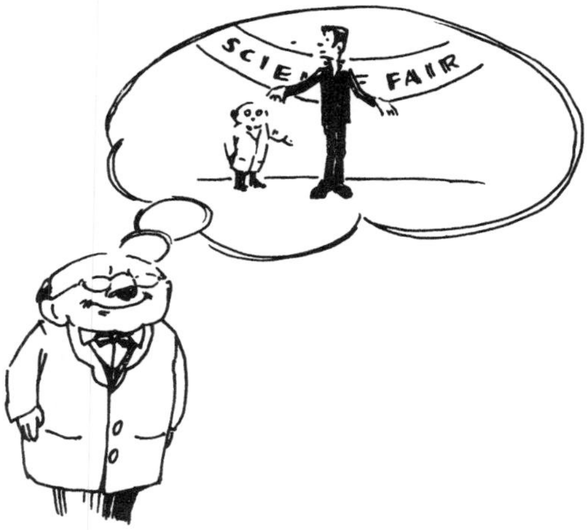

What materials will you use?

What is supposed to happen? What do you predict will happen?

How will you display or report your results? Use the next page to draw your setup.

Name _____ Date _____

Draw your setup here.

Activity Sheet 9.2.

Writing with Invisible Ink

Try using this invisible ink recipe to write a secret science trivia answer to a question for this month. Use one of the current events trivia game cards, and write the question on the front side in regular ink. Then write the answer to the question in invisible ink. Switch cards with classmates, and try to figure out the answers!

Recipe for Invisible Ink

1. Combine 3 tablespoons of salt and 3 tablespoons of hot water, and stir to mix. *Use caution!*
2. Use a drinking straw or a writing feather quill to dip into the solution.
3. Write with the invisible ink on your trivia game card.
4. Allow to dry thoroughly until the writing disappears.

Procedure

Give your trivia game card with the invisible answer to a classmate. Let him or her answer the question orally. Then that person can decode the answer by carefully coloring over the paper with a soft lead pencil. Did he or she answer the question correctly? How about you? Did you answer that person's trivia card correctly?

277

Activity Sheet 9.3.

Investigating Caffeine

Caffeine is found in tea, coffee, and kola nuts (often used in soft drinks called colas). Look for differences in teas, coffees, and sodas; some are decaffeinated.

Vocabulary		
caffeine	blood pressure	metabolism

What does caffeine do to a living organism? Research caffeine and its effects in the library or on the Internet. Then put a check next to three of the following six statements that are true about caffeine:

_____ Caffeine speeds up a person's heart rate.

_____ Caffeine speeds up a person's metabolism.

_____ Caffeine slows a person's heart rate.

_____ Caffeine raises a person's blood pressure.

_____ Caffeine lowers a person's blood pressure.

_____ Caffeine slows a person's metabolism.

Look at the ingredients on several cans of soda. Write the information about one decaffeinated soda and one caffeinated soda on the cans shown on the next page.

What might you conclude about caffeine? Can drinking too many caffeinated soft drinks be harmful? Can you explain what caffeine does to your body that might make it harmful?

Soda with
caffeine

Decaffeinated
Soda

Activity Sheet 9.4.

Careers in Science

What are some career possibilities in science or in the medical field? Would you like to become a doctor, a geologist, a nurse, a chemist, or a researcher? Read about these fields. If possible, interview a person in one of these areas, and use the form on the next page to write notes about a science career of your choice. To learn more about careers in science and medicine, visit these Web sites:

www.nal.usda.gov/Kids/careers.htm

www.kids.gov/k_careers.htm

www.niehs.nih.gov/kids/labcoat.htm

Careers in Science *(Cont'd.)*

Field of Science: _____

Job Title: _____

Description of job: _____
_____
_____

Education or Training Required: _____
_____

Advantages of This Job: _____
_____

Disadvantages of This Job: _____
_____

Would you like a career in this field? Why or why not?
_____
_____
_____

Using your imagination, what would you like to do in this field of science that hasn't been done? (Use the back of this form.)

☆BONUS: Can you name one person in this field who has contributed greatly? Who is this person, and what did he or she do?

Aviation and Space Milestones

WORD BOX
Skylab I   Charles Lindberg
Amelia Earhart   Sally Ride
Edward White
Valentina Tereshkova

Read the names in the Word Box. Then write the correct name on the line next to the event or description of the aviation milestone. Research the words in the Word Box before beginning.

First Soviet woman to travel in space on June 16, 1963 in spacecraft *Vostok 6.*

First woman to fly alone across the Atlantic Ocean (from Newfoundland to Ireland in 1932).

First American woman in space (flew on the space shuttle *Challenger* in 1983).

First American to walk in space (from *Gemini 4* in 1965).

_____

First manned space station sent into space in 1973.

_____

First American pilot to successfully navigate his plane across the Atlantic Ocean, from New York to Paris in 1927.

_____

Activity Sheet 9.6.

Make Your Own Pickles!

Here is a recipe to make your own pickles. Pickling is a form of food preservation that requires putting a vegetable, such as a cucumber, in a vinegar solution combined with pickling salt or table salt that is not iodized. Pickling preserves food because the vinegar solution initiates the process of *fermentation*. Fermentation converts sugars into alcohol, which prevents undesirable microorganisms from developing or growing in a food or environment. When food starts to smell bad or grows moldy, it has become a breeding ground for undesirable microorganisms and should no longer be eaten. Fermentation prevents those microorganisms from growing in food because of the presence of alcohol.

Many recipes require that you "can" your pickles. The recipe given here can be made without the canning process, and the pickles can be enjoyed for months. For more information on how to make your own pickles and relishes, check out www.farmgal.tripod.com/PicklesRelish.html.

Do you know the signs and causes of "poor" pickles? Poor pickles are too soft or shriveled.

Make Your Own Pickles! *(Cont'd.)*

Recipe for Pickles

Caution: Knives and other slicing tools are dangerous; adult supervision required.

2 quarts fresh unwaxed cucumbers, washed well and sliced

2 fresh onions, peeled and thinly sliced

1-gallon storage container with a tight-fitting lid

Pickle solution:

4 cups high-grade cider vinegar with acidity of 40 to 60 grains

4 cups sugar

¼ teaspoon each of celery seed and powdered alum

1¼ teaspoon each of mustard seed and turmeric

⅓ cup uniodized table salt

1. Mix the pickle solution ingredients together well, and pour into the gallon container.

2. Add the sliced cucumbers and onions and layer them in the container.

3. Put on the airtight lid, and shake the container well (and carefully!). Then place the container in the refrigerator and leave undisturbed for 1 day.

4. On the next day and every day of the next week, shake the container several minutes and turn it upside down. Alternate the container's position every day for a week: one day with the top up and the next with the top down.

5. At the end of the week, the refrigerated pickles are ready to be enjoyed. Any uneaten pickles can be refrigerated for months.

Name _____   Date _____

Activity Sheet 9.7.

Summer Solstice

Read the words on the sun. Then use the words to fill in the blanks below. Be alert: one term is used for two statements!

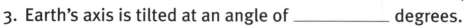

1. Earth revolves around the sun _____ a year or every _____ days.

2. Earth rotates or spins on its _____ once every _____ hours.

3. Earth's axis is tilted at an angle of _____ degrees.

4. _____ is the name of the force that helps keep Earth stable in its yearlong orbit around the sun.

5. Earth moves in a _____ direction, in a path shaped like an _____.

6. The north end of Earth's axis points toward the _____.

7. During _____, Earth is tilted toward the _____.

8. _____ is a word that means the sun stands at its greatest distance from the celestial equator.

9. During the summer solstice, it is summer in the _____. The North Pole is tilted at an angle of _____ degrees toward the sun.

285

Summer Solstice *(Cont'd.)*

Select four cities from four different parts of the world, and complete the chart below. Use the Internet as your information source.

Note: The solstice occurs twice a year: on or about June 21 (when Earth's tilt positions the Northern Hemisphere toward the sun) and on or about December 21 (when Earth's tilt positions the Northern Hemisphere away from the sun). When it is summer in the Northern Hemisphere, it is winter in the Southern Hemisphere, and vice versa.

First Day of Summer: _____ Year: _____

CITY	WEATHER	HIGH TEMPERATURE	LOW TEMPERATURE	RECORD HIGH FOR THIS DAY
1.				
2.				
3.				
4.				

Draw four dots on the maps to show where your cities are located on the globe.

MAY-JUNE

1 MAY: Happy May Day! Plan a Science Fair using Activity Sheet 9.3.

2

3 JUNE: Ed White walked in space.

4 MAY: Write an invisible message today using Activity Sheet 9.3.

5 MAY: First American in space in 1961. Cheers for Alan Shepard Jr.

6

MAY-JUNE

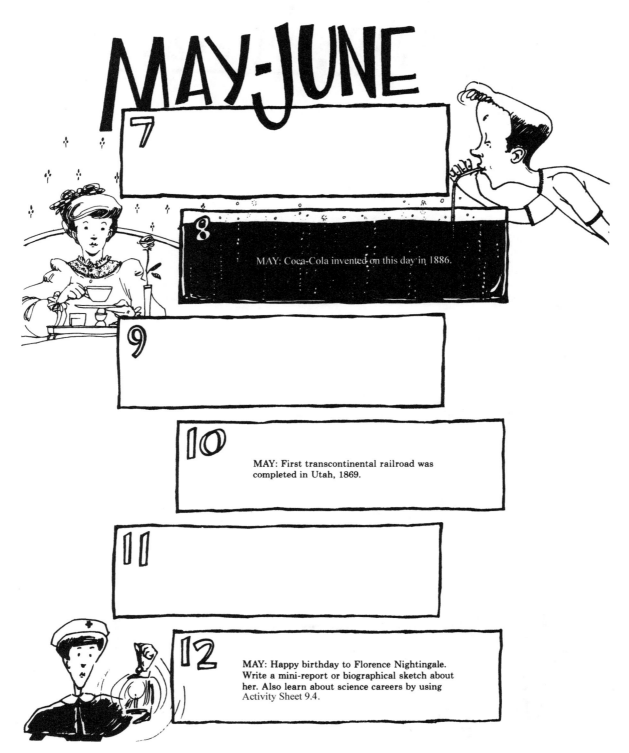

7

8 MAY: Coca-Cola invented on this day in 1886.

9

10 MAY: First transcontinental railroad was completed in Utah, 1869.

11

12 MAY: Happy birthday to Florence Nightingale. Write a mini-report or biographical sketch about her. Also learn about science careers by using Activity Sheet 9.4.

MAY·JUNE

13

14
MAY: First manned space station, *Skylab I*, launched in 1973.

15
MAY: International Pickle Week is the third week of May. Make pickles by following the directions on Activity Sheet 9.6.
JUNE: Happy birthday to Arkansas.

16
JUNE: First woman in space, Valentina Tereshkova.

17

18
JUNE: First U.S. woman in space, Sally Ride, was aboard the space shuttle *Challenger* in 1983.

MAY-JUNE

19

20 MAY: Who was the first woman to fly solo across the Atlantic Ocean (in 1932)? Write a biographical sketch on this famous woman. Another space milestone: What was the *Spirit of St. Louis*? JUNE: Happy birthday, William Hewlett.

21 JUNE: First day of summer arrives. Do Activity Sheet 9.7 to learn more about the solstice, the seasons, and weather.

22

23

24

290

MAY-JUNE

25

JUNE: A U.S. all-time high for June was set in Death Valley, California, in 2006. How hot did it get? Play the trivia game to find out.

26

27

28

29

30/31

Appendix 1
Answer Key

September

1.4. What Do You Know About Mosquitoes?

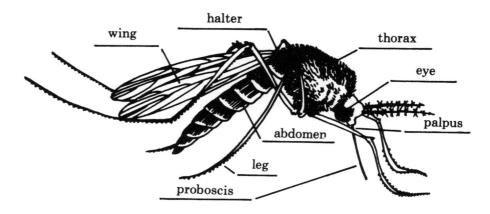

1.6. How Do Insects Communicate?

Definitions

Entomology: the study of insects

Entomologist: a person who studies insects

Pheromones: a chemical that some animals release to attract animals
of the same kind or species or to ward off other animals

1.8. The Story of Chocolate, an Amazing Journey

Definitions

Fermentation: a process whereby a substance is changed chemically by yeast, mold, or bacteria

Winnowing: a process used to separate or sort out

Nib: the inside of the cacao bean, often ground

Conching ("KONK-ing"): mixing chocolate with heavy rollers

October

2.1. National Child Health Day

Path to take: 1. polyunsaturated; 2. false; 3. true; 4. poultry or fish; 5. true; 6. baking or broiling

2.3. Basic Food Groups

Across	Down
2. apple	1. carbohydrate
4. fish	3. liver
6. hamburger	4. fig
7. protein	5. butter

2.8. Why Migration?

Mixed-up words: eel, hummingbird, gray bat, Canada geese, salmon, monarch butterfly, warbler, gray whale

2.10. The Microscope and the Amoeba

1. nucleus
2. cell membrane
3. food vacuole
4. contractile vacuole

2.11. Standard Time

Central: 4:00   Mountain: 3:00   Central: 10:00

Fill-in blanks: 24; 1; 4; yes

November

3.2. Nutrition in Space

freeze-dried—vacuum drying in a frozen state

natural—original form

thermostabilized—cooked at moderate temperatures and sealed in cans

intermediate moisture process—removing part of water

irradiated—preserved by exposure

dehydrated—water removed

3.3. Exploring Saturn's Largest Moon

Across
1. Titan
3. Methane
7. Giant

Down
2. Ice
4. Cassini
5. Nitrogen
6. Region

3.4. Investigating Spacecraft

Mercury

measurements: 9.5 feet long; 6 feet wide at base

interior space: 36 cubic feet

seating capacity: 1

Gemini

measurements: 11 feet long; 7.5 feet wide at base

interior space: 50 cubic feet

seating capacity: 2

Apollo

measurements: 11 feet long; 12.8 feet wide at base (also, service module of 24 feet by 13 feet; and lunar module of 22.9 feet by 11 feet)

interior space: 210 cubic feet (also lunar module of 157 cubic feet)

seating capacity: 3

3.5. Be a Lunar Rockhound
1. breccia
2. igneous
3. spinel
4. feldspar
5. anorthosite

3.7. Star Match

1	Sirius (–1.46) Blue-white star	Lyra (The Harp)
4	Alpha Centauri (–.27) Yellow-white star	Canis Major (The Big Dog)
5	Vega (.03) Blue-white	Centaurus (Centaur)
2	Canopus (–.72) White	Orion (The Hunter)
3	Arcturus (–.04) Orange	Carina (The Keel)
6	Capella (.08) Yellow-white	Auriga (The Charioteer)
7	Rigel (.12) Blue	Böotes (The Herdsman)

3.8. Aerobics in Space?

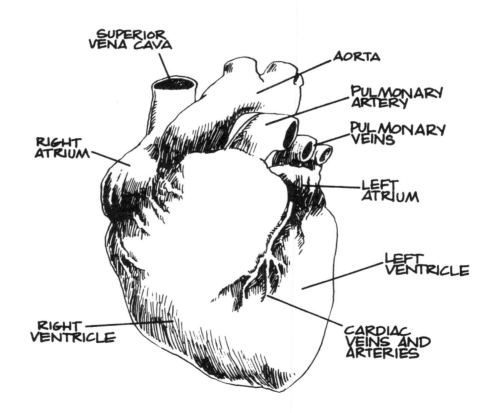

SUPERIOR VENA CAVA
AORTA
PULMONARY ARTERY
PULMONARY VEINS
RIGHT ATRIUM
LEFT ATRIUM
LEFT VENTRICLE
RIGHT VENTRICLE
CARDIAC VEINS AND ARTERIES

3.9. Celsius Degrees

250°F = 121.11°C

–250°F = 156.67°C

Day 1 = 37°C

Day 2 = 37.39°C

Day 3 = 39.17°C

December

4.2. Will This Food Last Forever?

beefsteak—8 to 12 months

fish—6 to 9 months

butter—3 to 6 months

whipped cream—3 months

lobster—1 month

turkey—6 months

frosted cake—2 months

doughnuts—2 to 4 weeks

4.3. Winners of the Nobel Prize

Across

3. X ray
5. cholesterol
6. Nobel

Down

1. physiology
2. ear
4. insulin
5. cat

4.4. Be a Stargazer

1. Leo
2. Cygnus
3. Orion

4. Lyra
5. Pegasus

4.7. Remembering Edison

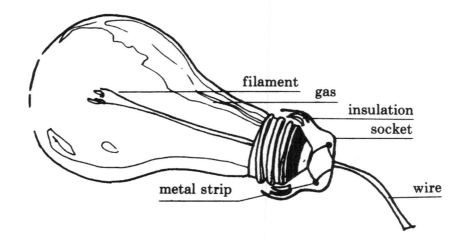

January
5.3. Did You Hear That? Detecting Differences in Pitch
1. d; 2. a; 3. c; 4. b

February
6.4. The Earthworm

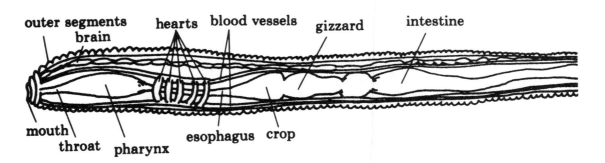

Only item 4 is false; all the rest are true.

6.5. A Who's Who of Desert Animals

6.6. Animals of the Grand Canyon

6.7. Animals and Their Burrows
bumblebee; prairie dog; elf owl; groundhog; kangaroo rat; earthworm

6.8. Leap Year
The leap years are 2000, 1980, 1776, 1600, 1588, 1492, 800, and 476.

March

7.1. Investigating Flowers and Their Parts

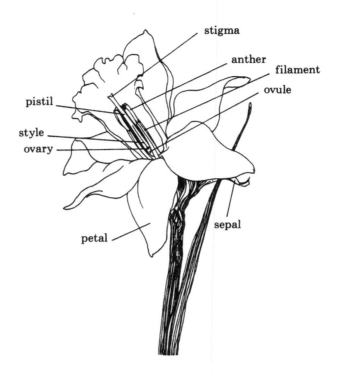

7.2. Trees in Our National Parks and Around the World

Yellowstone National Park
1. Montana, Idaho, Wyoming (any two)
2. Old Faithful
3. A geyser is a spring that erupts, spewing heated water and steam.

Mount Rainier National Park
1. Washington
2. examples: bison, elk, bear, coyote, sheep, bobcat, mountain lion
3. Cascades
4. Moisture

Map Locations
1. Yosemite (California)
2. Everglades (Florida)
3. Great Smoky Mountains (North Carolina, Tennessee)
4. Acadia (Maine)

7.3. Salutes to Florida and Vermont

Across
1. palm
3. deer
4. alligator
8. maple
9. moss
11. Vermont

Down
2. Florida
5. sunshine
6. liana
7. coconut
10. Green
12. sap

7.4. What's in an Apple?

Across
1. dormant
4. Appleseed
8. autumn
9. root

Down
2. apple
3. Chapman
5. pollination
6. spring
7. dwarf
10. brown

7.6. What Is Light Refraction?

1. red
2. true
3. true
4. true
5. prism, air

7.7. St. Patrick's Day and the Shamrock

Across
2. alfalfa
3. green
5. shamrock
8. Patrick

Down
1. beans
4. legumes
6. clover
7. snakes

April

8.1. Let's Save Lots of Watts!

The most energy-efficient bulb is bulb B.

8.3. What Can We Recycle?

biodegradable: capable of being readily decomposed

nonbiodegradable: not able to be decomposed

returnable: refillable; if a deposit has been paid, the deposit is refunded when the container is returned *recyclable:* capable of being used again in the same form or in a different form

reusable: capable of being used again in the same form

Illustration Labels

paper bag: biodegradable, recyclable, reusable

soda can: returnable, recyclable

plastic bag: nonbiodegradable, recyclable, reusable

chicken bones: biodegradable

newspaper: biodegradable, recyclable

glass bottle: nonbiodegradable, returnable, recyclable, reusable

apple core: biodegradable

plastic jug: nonbiodegradable, recyclable, reusable

disposable diaper: some biodegradable, some nonbiodegradable

8.4. How Can We Help Our National Parks?

Forest conservation: 1, 2, 5, 7

Wildlife conservation: 3, 4, 6, 7

8.6. Making Our Water Safe

All of the animals in the illustration should be circled.

8.9. Endangered Species

1. Black-capped vireo
2. Northern aplomado falcon
3. Florida panther
4. Schaus swallowtail butterfly
5. Aleutian Canada goose
6. Red-cockaded woodpecker
7. whooping crane
8. American crocodile
9. Eastern indigo snake
10. small whorled pogonia
11. gila trout
12. running buffalo clover

May–June

9.3. Investigating Caffeine
Statements to be checked off are the first, second, and fourth.

9.5. Aviation and Space Milestones
Valentina Tereshkova

Amelia Earhart

Sally Ride

Edward White

Skylab I

Charles Lindbergh

9.7. Summer Solstice
1. once; 365¼
2. axis; 24
3. 23½
4. Gravity
5. clockwise; ellipse
6. North Star
7. summer; sun
8. Solstice
9. Northern Hemisphere; 23½

Appendix 2
Ordering Information for Materials

Correlated Videos

All correlated videos (Appendix 3) may be ordered directly from

Phoenix Learning Group
2349 Chaffee Drive
St. Louis, MO 63146
(800) 221-1274; fax (314) 569-2834
phoenixlearninggroup.com

The videos and DVDs listed in Appendix 3 are optional. Each has been reviewed and can be referenced for a complete description and school-level correlation in the Phoenix Learning Group catalogue. Consult the catalogue or call for information regarding current rental or purchase prices.

Science Equipment and Materials

Most of the equipment, live specimens, prepared microscopic slides, and teaching charts and materials listed here can be ordered from

Connecticut Valley Biological Supply Co.
P.O. Box 326
82 Valley Road
Southampton, MA 01073
(800) 628-7748; fax (413) 527-4030
www.ctvalleybio.com

Call or write for a complete catalogue. The following list of materials and products is correlated to the monthly activities in this book. These are not required materials, but they might enrich your program. Other biological supply houses you might visit online as ordering sites are www.sargentwelch.com and www.sciencekit.com.

September
Mold Study Set (prepared microscope slides)

Mosquito Life History (plastic mount)

October
Amoeba Proteus (prepared microscope slide)

Cells of Your Body (cheek cells, smear, stained)

Amoeba (live slide set)

Mixed Protozoa (prepared microscope slides)

Scientific Visual Specialists Charts: Amoeba

Microscope (computer lab simulation from Cross Educational Software)

November

Solar System (chart, *Voyager* data)

Charts: Solar System, Map of the Moon

Wall-Sized Star Charts: The Full Earth (*Apollo 17*)

Good Heavens! (astronomical trivia game)

Stellar 28 (games)

Circulation Game and Circulatory System (model)

Introduction Life Science Series: Human Body System (charts)

Drugs and Heartbeat: Experiments with a Daphnia (computer simulation program)

December

Astronomy Study Prints

January

An Introduction to Rocks and Minerals (VHS full-motion video)

Minerals of the World (color poster)

February

Animal Rummy Cards: North American Wildlife

Earthworm Set (model)

Earthworm (model)

The Earthworm: Computer Dissection Program

Live Earthworms

Animal Tracks of New England (chart)

March

Flower (model)

Typical Dicot Flower (model)

Flower: Lily (model)

Food Webs and Food Chain (games)

The Pollination Game

Introduction Life Science Series: Plant Parts Set (charts)

Plant Growth and Development Set (charts)

Flowers for Dissection (fresh): Gladiolus, Miniature Lilies

Seeds for Germination: Clover

April
Animal Rummy Cards: Endangered Species
Environmental Rummy

May–June
Sky Challenger (games and activities)

In addition to the computer simulations listed here, there are other computer programs that you may want to order for your science curriculum. These can be ordered directly from

Cross Educational Software
P.O. Box 1536
Ruston, LA 71270
(800) 768-1969

Call or write for a complete catalogue. Sample programs include

Spell-A-Vision (Add your own science vocabulary words!)
Create-A-Test (many selections including, Biology 640: Ecology and Biology 647: Vertebrates)

Books

These books may be ordered to enrich the activities in this book or other school and library programs, K–6:

Moutran, J. S. *The Story of Punxsutawney Phil.* Farmington, Conn.: Literary Publications, 1987.

Moutran, J. S. *Collecting Bugs and Things.* Los Angeles: Price Stern Sloan, 1988.

Moutran, J. S. *Elementary Science Activities for All Seasons.* West Nyack, N.Y.: Center for Applied Research in Education, 1990.

Moutran, J. S. *Will Spring Ever Come to Gobbler's Knob?* Farmington, Conn.: Literary Publications, 1992.

NASA Space Materials

For teacher resource and free teaching materials about space exploration to correlate with activities for November and May–June, including reproducible materials and charts, contact NASA at www.nasa.gov or www.spacecenter.org.

Appendix 3
Correlated Science Videos and DVDs

The following DVDs and VHS videos are available from www.Teachers MediaCompany.com, 800-262-8837, a division of Sunburst Visual, 2 Sky-line Drive, Suite 101, Hawthorne, NY 10532-2130. In most cases, DVD format is listed, but VHS is available as well. Check online or with the company for your ordering needs, or for the video order number.

September

Title	Grades	Format	Order Prefix	Order Code
The Earth's Position and Seasons	3–12	DVD	TBTG	355612
Climate & Seasons Video Quiz	5–9	Both	TBTG	370630
Earth's Seasons	4–12	VHS	TBTG	352976
Our Amazing Solar System	5+	DVD	TBTG	525619
Welcome to Maps	7–12	DVD	TBTG	389632
Mars: Dead or Alive	7–12	DVD	TBTG	362563
California Desert & Coast	1–8	DVD	TBTG	385285
Inventions, Overview	3–12	DVD	TBTG	356356
Electric Light, Edison	3–12	DVD	TBTG	355813
Viral Emergence	3–12	DVD	TBTG	358831
Infectious Diseases	3–12	DVD	TBTG	356311
Viruses Video Quiz	4–10	DVD	TBTG	345764
Weather & Climate	3–5	DVD	TBTG	364309
Heat & Weather	3–12	DVD	TBTG	356152
Insect Life Cycle's Metamorphosis	1–5	DVD	TBTG	346198
Insects	3–12	VHS	TBTG	353078
Butterfly & Moth	3–12	VHS	TBTG	353765
Light Video Quiz	5–9	Both	TBTG	344057
Refraction	3–12	DVD	TBTG	358612
Light	5–9	DVD	TBTG	372949
Light	3–5	VHS	TBTG	354553
Magnetism Video Quiz	4–10	Both	TBTG	344144
Magnetic Force/Magnetism	3–5	DVD	TBTG	354436
Magnetism	5–12	DVD	TBTG	344141
Electromagnets	3–12	DVD	TBTG	356563
Antibiotics	3–12	DVD	TBTG	355306
Germs at Work	3–12	DVD	TBTG	356143
Introduction to Bacteria	3–12	DVD	TBTG	356302
Molds	3–12	DVD	TBTG	356626
Tiny Talents: Beneficial Bacteria	3–12	DVD	TBTG	358678
Atoms Video Quiz	3–6	Both	TBTG	341597
Electricity Video Quiz	4–10	Both	TBTG	342848

October

Title	Grades	Format	Order Prefix	Order Code
Nutrition	3–12	DVD	TBTG	356743
Human Nutrition Video Quiz	5–9	DVD	TBTG	342431
Fire	3–12	DVD	TBTG	355963
Fantastic Food Pyramid	4–9	DVD	TBTG	391117
Intro to Cells	3–12	DVD	TBTG	356305
Cells	5–12	DVD	TBTG	370855
Gravity Affects Everything	3–12	DVD	TBTG	356065
Birds Video	4–10	Both	TBTG	341783
Cells Video Quiz	5–9	Both	TBTG	341978
Inside a Cell	5–9	Both	TBTG	372507
How to Use a Microscope	6–12	VHS	TBTG	360185

November

Title	Grades	Format	Order Prefix	Order Code
Space Facts	5 & up	VHS	TBTG	363935
Voyage into Space	3–5	DVD	TBTG	376342
The Moon	3–12	DVD	TBTG	373432
NASA Space Station	K–5	VHS	TBTG	366674
Clouds Video Quiz	3–6	Both	TBTG	370504
Plants Video Quiz	4–10	Both	TBTG	344657
Solar System: Outer Gas Planets	4–9	VHS	TBTG	337207
America in Space Video Quiz	4–10	Both	TBTG	341519
Rocks & Minerals	3–12	DVD	TBTG	351754
Forces & Gravity Video Quiz	4–10	Both	TBTG	343043
Stargazing	3–6	DVD	TBTG	354614
The Stars	3–5	Both	TBTG	375463
Exploring Stars	3–6	DVD	TBTG	305194
Plants in Space	3–12	DVD	TBTG	358339

December

Title	Grades	Format	Order Prefix	Order Code
Thomas Edison	7+	VHS	TBTG	339523
Wright Brothers	1–5	VHS	TBTG	342034
Inventions & Innovations	7+	VHS	TBTG	598432
Scientists & Inventors	6–12	DVD	TBTG	390129
Inventors Video Quiz	3–8	DVD	TBTG	343757
Meet the Great Inventors	5–9	DVD	TBTG	343277
Edison, Electric Light	3–12	DVD	TBTG	355813
Whitney, Cotton Gin	3–12	DVD	TBTG	355528

January

Title	Grades	Format	Order Prefix	Order Code
Balloons	7+	VHS	TBTG	340285
Atoms Video Quiz	3–6	Both	TBTG	369796
States of Matter Video Quiz	4–10	Both	TBTG	345239
Common Properties of Matter	3–6	DVD	TBTG	346150
Matter	4–8	DVD	TBTG	351673
Sound Video Quiz	4–10	Both	TBTG	345260
Understanding Sound	4–8	DVD	TBTG	351802
Rock Cycle Video Quiz	5–12	Both	TBTG	345005
Rocks & Minerals Video Quiz	4–10	Both	TBTG	344918
Rocks & Minerals	4–8	VHS	TBTG	353840
Rocks & Minerals	4–8	DVD	TBTG	351754

February

Title	Grades	Format	Order Prefix	Order Code
Desert—Land of Extremes	7–12	DVD	TBTG	383848
Desert	4–8	VHS	TBTG	353777
Desert Biomes	4–8	VHS	TBTG	354773
Grand Canyon	3–12	DVD	TBTG	356047
California: Desert Coast	1–8	DVD	TBTG	385285

March

Title	Grades	Format	Order Prefix	Order Code
Thrilling Experiments: Plants	5–9	Both	TBTG	374902
Flowers, Plants & Trees	3–8	DVD	TBTG	351590
Florida: A Unique Ecosystem	1–8	DVD	TBTG	385291
Tree	4–8	VHS	TBTG	353867
Weather: Clouds & Reflected Sunlight	3–12	DVD	TBTG	355609
Photosynthesis: Leaves in the Process	3–12	DVD	TBTG	356521
Chloroplasts	3–12	DVD	TBTG	357172
Cells: Chloroplasts, Chlorophyll, Photosynthesis	3–12	DVD	TBTG	355486
Light: The Spectrum Refraction	3–12	DVD	TBTG	358612

April

Title	Grades	Format	Order Prefix	Order Code
Hubble Telescope	3–12	DVD	TBTG	356266
Recycling: Garbologists	3–12	DVD	TBTG	358435
Recycling: The Earth as a Recycler	3–12	DVD	TBTG	358414
Air Pollution, Smog & Acid Rain	4–12	VHS	TBTG	355603
People & Their Environment	3–6	DVD	TBTG	354563

May–June

Title	Grades	Format	Order Prefix	Order Code
How to Prepare a Science Fair Project	5–9	DVD	TBTG	354518
Science Fair Projects	1–6	DVD	TBTG	348019
The Earth's Position & Seasons	3–12	DVD	TBTG	355612
The Sun: Seasons	3–6	DVD	TBTG	358594

Appendix 4
Correlated
Computer Software

In addition to the software recommended in Appendix 2, the following companies offer computer software in science that can be used to reinforce concepts and skills introduced in this book. Call or write for a free catalogue:

Sunburst Communications
39 Washington Avenue
Pleasantville, NY 10570
(800) 431-1934

Wings for Learning
1600 Greenhills Road
P.O. Box 660002
Scotts Valley, CA 95067
(800) 321-7511

The computer software listed below by month is correlated with the activities in this book. All are sold by Sunburst or Wings for Learning.

September

Bank Street School Filer: Climate and Weather Databases

Learn About Insects

October

Discover

Food for Thought

The Voyage of the *Mimi* (Maps and Navigation)

The Second Voyage of the *Mimi*

November

Bank Street School Filer:

    Climate and Weather Databases

    Astronomy Database

    Space Database

    Minerals Database

The Human Pump

Learning to Cope with Pressure

The Smoking Decision

Planetary Construction Set

Sir Isaac Newton's Games

The Second Voyage of the *Mimi*

January

Playing with Science: Temperature
Hands On: Temperature
Exploring Science: Temperature
The Incredible Laboratory
Playing with Science: Motion
Bank Street School Filer: Minerals Database

February

Animal Trackers
Safari Search
Exploring Tidepools
Bank Street School Filer: Animal Life Databases
The Voyage of the *Mimi* (Whales and Their Environment)
Learn About Animals

March

Botanical Gardens
The Voyage of the *Mimi* (Ecosystems)
Learn About Plants
What Shape Is That Color?

April

Bank Street School Filer: Endangered Species Databases
The Voyage of the *Mimi* (Ecosystems)
Exploring Tidepools

May/June

The following are available at www.TeacherMediaCompany.com, 1-800-262-8837.

How to Prepare a Science Fair Project
Science Fair Projects
The Earth's Position and Seasons
The Sun: Seasons

The following interactive videodiscs are available from Coronet/MTI Film and Video, (800) 621-2131, in its Discovery Channel Interactive Videodisc Library Programs and can be used with various activities in this book:

Insects, Little Giants of the Earth, LA-DIL 203
Investigating History: Treasures from the Deep, LA-DIL 201
Investigating Science: Treasures from the Deep, LA-DIL 202

Appendix 5
Science Trivia Game

PLANTS & ANIMALS

Q:

A:

INVENTORS & INVENTIONS

Q:

A:

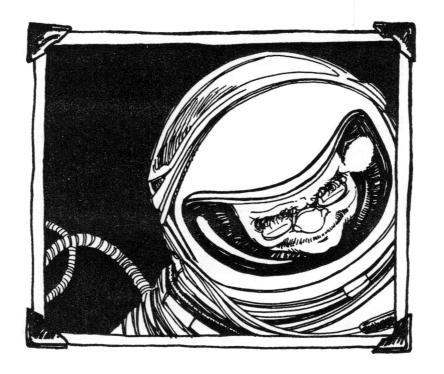

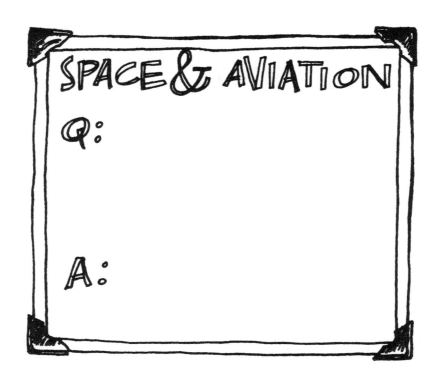

SPACE & AVIATION

Q:

A:

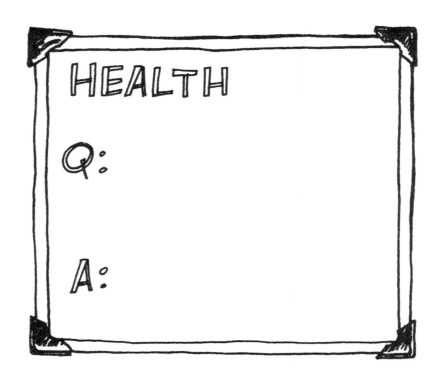

HEALTH

Q:

A:

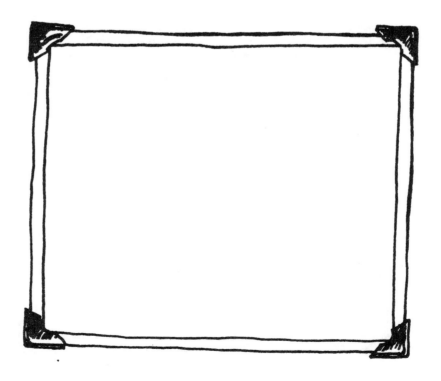

326

For each monthly trivia game, select the questions that you want your students to answer. The reproducible cards precede these questions and answers. The questions can be printed on the chalkboard, together with the answers. Or students can cut out the questions and answers and paste them on the backs of their cards according to category. Here's how to play.

One student selects a question card with the picture side up. Another reads the card question aloud (on the reverse side of the picture card) and gets three chances to answer the question. After the third try, another person gets a chance, or the answer is supplied by the student, and the card goes into the question pile again. There are blank cards for current events, where students make their own questions and answers for the month, depending on what is happening in the world. The person with the most points is the "Superscientist of the Month"!

Scoring

Correct answer on first try	5 points
Correct answer on second try	3 points
Correct answer on third try	1 point

Monthly Trivia Cards: Questions and Answers

Feel free to create your own trivia cards based on your school curriculum and texts or findings from students' mini-reports and biographical sketches.

September Questions and Answers

Card: Space and Aviation

Q: The early history of this planet was much like Earth's. It once had water and shares the same sun as Earth. This planet was visited by *Viking 1* and *Viking 2* (September 3, 1976). Name the planet.

A: Mars

Card: Inventors and Inventions

Q: Who was the inventor of the electric lightbulb?

A: Thomas Edison

Card: Plants and Animals

Q: This large western state (third in area) is famous for its avocados. Which state celebrates its statehood on September 9?

A: California

Card: Inventors and Inventions
Q: Who invented the first sewing machine (1846)?
A: Elias Howe

Card: Inventors and Inventions
Q: This famous dam operated its first hydroelectric generator on September 11, 1936. Name the dam.
A: Hoover Dam

Card: Space and Aviation
Q: The first spacecraft to land on the moon was launched from the Soviet Union on September 12, 1959. Name the spacecraft.
A: *Luna 2*

Card: Health
Q: The world's record for the hottest day was set in El Azizia, Libya, on September 13, 1922. How hot did it get?
A: 136°F

Card: Health
Q: Name the famous American pathologist who helped identify the cause of yellow fever by discovering that a mosquito was the carrier of the disease.
A: Walter Reed

Card: Plants and Animals
Q: A Russian Nobel Prize winner, Ivan Pavlov, was born on September 14, 1849. He taught an animal to salivate when it heard a bell ring by first teaching the pet to salivate with food. What kind of animal did he teach?
A: A dog

Card: Space and Aviation
Q: How fast is the speed of light?
A: 186,000 miles per second

Card: Miscellaneous
Q: What is the name of the natural magnet containing iron?
A: Lodestone

Card: Space and Aviation
Q: Earth spins on its axis and rotates around the sun. When the path of the sun crosses the equator and there are twelve hours each of sunlight and darkness on Earth, what do we call that day, which occurs twice a year?
A: The equinox

Card: Health
Q: Who were the first people to produce penicillin?
A: Howard Florey and Ernst Chain

Card: Inventors and Inventions
Q: Who invented an instrument used to detect and measure radiation? The instrument is named after its inventor.
A: Hans Geiger

Card: Miscellaneous
Q: When electrons move in the same direction, what do we call this type of electric current?
A: DC (direct current)

October Questions and Answers

Card: Space and Aviation
Q: What was the name of the first artificial satellite that was launched into space (in 1957)?
A: *Sputnik 1*

Card: Miscellaneous
Q: What is the national flower of the United States?
A: The rose

Card: Plants and Animals
Q: The Great Chicago Fire (October 8, 1871) may have been started by an animal kicking over an oil lantern inside a barn. What animal in Mrs. O'Leary's barn may have done that?
A: A cow

Card: Inventors and Inventions
Q: What instrument helped Columbus navigate the seas and ultimately discover the New World on October 12, 1492?
A: The compass

Card: Space and Aviation
Q: What was the name of one of the first commercial airships? It looked like a huge balloon.
A: A zeppelin

Card: Health

Q: What is the name of the medical drugs used to eliminate pain during surgery?
A: Anesthetics

Card: Inventors and Inventions

Q: Who founded the National Wildlife Federation?
A: J. N. "Ding" Darling

Card: Inventors and Inventions

Q: Who invented the first microscope?
A: Antoni van Leeuwenhoek

Card: Miscellaneous

Q: What famous canal connects the Hudson River to Lake Erie?
A: Erie Canal

Card: Inventors and Inventions

Q: What is the name of the synthetic yarn invented by Wallace Carrothers at the DuPont plant in 1938?
A: Nylon

Card: Miscellaneous

Q: What famous statue, a symbol of freedom, was given to the U.S. by France and dedicated in New York in 1886?
A: The Statue of Liberty

Card: Miscellaneous

Q: What state (the thirty-sixth state) celebrates its statehood on October 31?
A: Nevada

Card: Miscellaneous

Q: What is the name of the standard of time that ends in October?
A: Daylight saving time; it begins on the first Sunday in April and ends on the last Sunday in October.

November Questions and Answers
Card: Inventors and Inventions

Q: When the U.S. Weather Bureau made its first forecasts in 1870, what instrument did it use to broadcast the news?
A: The telegraph

Card: Space and Aviation
Q: What was the name of the first dog in space (*Sputnik 2*, 1957)?
A: Laika

Card: Miscellaneous
Q: What was the name of the boy king whose tomb was discovered in Egypt in 1922?
A: King Tutankhamen

Card: Inventors and Inventions
Q: Who was the scientist famous for research on radioactivity and the discovery of radium?
A: Marie Curie

Card: Inventors and Inventions
Q: Who was the scientist who first split the uranium nucleus?
A: Lise Meitner

Card: Space and Aviation
Q: What was the name of the second phase of NASA's space program employing two-manned spacecrafts and aimed at reaching the moon?
A: Project *Gemini*

Card: Space and Aviation
Q: The *Mariner 9* approached this planet in 1971. Name the planet.
A: Mars

Card: Space and Aviation
Q: What was the name of the second spacecraft to land on the moon (November 14, 1969) and return with large samples of moon rock?
A: *Apollo 12*

Card: Health
Q: What is the name of the muscular body organ that rhythmically contracts and circulates blood through the body?
A: The heart

Card: Inventors and Inventions
Q: Who invented the temperature scale that is based on 0° as the freezing point of water and 100° as the boiling point of water?
A: Anders Celsius

December Questions and Answers

Card: Health
Q: What is the name of the doctor who directed the team of surgeons for the first human heart transplant (December 3, 1967)?
A: Christiaan Barnard

Card: Inventors and Inventions
Q: Who invented the cotton gin?
A: Eli Whitney

Card: Inventors and Inventions
Q: Who invented dynamite?
A: Alfred Nobel

Card: Miscellaneous
Q: What is the name of the prize awarded in Stockholm and Oslo for physics, medicine and physiology, chemistry, peace, literature, and economic science each November 10?
A: The Nobel Prize

Card: Miscellaneous
Q: Name the anthropologist who wrote more than twenty-three books about people of different cultures.
A: Margaret Mead

Card: Space and Aviation
Q: Who were the famous brothers who flew the first airplane, in Kitty Hawk, North Carolina, on December 17, 1903?
A: Orville and Wilbur Wright

Card: Inventors and Inventions
Q: What was the name of the first almanac, published by Benjamin Franklin and issued on December 19, 1732?
A: *Poor Richard's Almanack*

Card: Space and Aviation
Q: Who broadcast this famous radio message from the U.S. space satellite *Atlas* on December 19, 1958: "To all mankind, America's wish for peace on Earth and goodwill toward men everywhere"?
A: President Dwight D. Eisenhower

Card: Space and Aviation

Q: What is the name of the first day of winter, the shortest day of the year?

A: The winter solstice

Card: Plants and Animals

Q: Name two plants that are associated with December.

A: Poinsettia, mistletoe, holly

Card: Health

Q: Name the "angel of the battlefield," the founder of the American Red Cross.

A: Clara Barton

Card: Inventors and Inventions

Q: Name the scientist who is credited with the discovery of pasteurization.

A: Louis Pasteur

Card: Space and Aviation

Q: Name the astronomer who discovered that Earth and the other planets revolve around the sun in an elliptical pattern. He is called the father of modern astronomy, and he was born in 1571.

A: Johannes Kepler

Card: Space and Aviation

Q: Name the scientist who is considered the founder of the science of aerodynamics and who built the first glider that could transport a person.

A: George Cayley

Card: Inventors and Inventions

Q: Who invented chewing gum?

A: William Semple

Card: Inventors and Inventions

Q: Who is the chemist who invented bonding rubber to fabric to make raincoats?

A: Charles Macintosh

January Questions and Answers

Card: Miscellaneous

Q: Who is the famous midnight rider, American patriot, and eyeglass maker born on December 1, 1735?

A: Paul Revere

Card: Miscellaneous
Q: Four states celebrate their admission to the Union during January. Name one of them.
A: Alaska, Utah, New Mexico, Michigan

Card: Inventors and Inventions
Q: Who invented a system of reading and writing for the blind?
A: Louis Braille

Card: Space and Aviation
Q: On January 7, 1785, two people crossed the English Channel by hot-air balloon flight. Name them.
A: John Jeffries and Jean-Pierre Blanchard

Card: Inventors and Inventions
Q: Who is the famous American composer remembered on January 13?
A: Stephen Foster

Card: Inventors and Inventions
Q: Name the famous scientist who was born on January 17, 1706.
A: Ben Franklin

Card: Inventors and Inventions
Q: Who invented the steam engine?
A: James Watt

Card: Inventors and Inventions
Q: Who invented storing food in tin cans (one of two people)?
A: Thomas Kensett, Ezra Daggett

Card: Miscellaneous
Q: Name the element that was discovered at Sutter's Mill, California, on January 24, 1848.
A: Gold

Card: Inventors and Inventions
Q: Name the famous composer who was born on January 27, 1756.
A: Wolfgang Mozart

Card: Inventors and Inventions

Q: Who developed the steamboat in the eighteenth century?

A: John Fitch

February Questions and Answers

Card: Inventors and Inventions

Q: Who built the world's first motion picture studio in West Orange, New Jersey, in 1893?

A: Thomas Edison

Card: Plants and Animals

Q: What hibernating animal emerges from its burrow on or about February 2?

A: Groundhog

Card: Space and Aviation

Q: Which spacecraft landed on the moon carrying astronauts Alan Shepard and Edgar D. Mitchell (February 4, 1971)?

A: *Apollo 14*

Card: Plants and Animals

Q: What organization concerned with wildlife was founded on February 5, 1936?

A: National Wildlife Federation

Card: Plants and Animals

Q: Name the famous naturalist who was fascinated by earthworms.

A: Charles Darwin

Card: Plants and Animals

Q: Are earthworms cold- or warm-blooded animals?

A: Cold blooded

Card: Miscellaneous

Q: Name two states that celebrate their statehood in February.

A: Colorado and Arizona

Card: Plants and Animals

Q: According to legend, what animals choose their mates on or about February 14?

A: Birds

Card: Space and Aviation

Q: Name the famous astronomer born on February 15, 1564.

A: Galileo

Card: Plants and Animals

Q: Name the famous national park that contains one of the seven wonders of the world.

A: Grand Canyon National Park

Card: Miscellaneous

Q: What is the name of the special year when February has 29 days instead of 28?

A: Leap Year

March Questions and Answers

Card: Plants and Animals

Q: What is the flower of the month of March?

A: Daffodil (jonquil)

Card: Plants and Animals

Q: Name one of three female parts of a flower.

A: Stigma, style, ovary

Card: Plants and Animals

Q: Name one of three male parts of a flower.

A: Stamen, anther, filament

Card: Plants and Animals

Q: Name the famous national park established by Congress on March 1, 1872.

A: Yellowstone National Park

Card: Miscellaneous

Q: Name two states that celebrate their statehood in March.

A: Florida and Vermont

Card: Plants and Animals
Q: Name the famous national park that Congress established on March 2, 1899.
A: Mount Rainier National Park

Card: Space and Aviation
Q: Name the planet that was discovered on March 13, 1781, by Sir William Herschel.
A: Uranus

Card: Space and Aviation
Q: What is the name of the first day of spring?
A: Vernal equinox

Card: Space and Aviation
Q: What does the word *equinox* mean?
A: Equal night

Card: Plants and Animals
Q: Who was the legendary man who traveled the country planting apple seeds?
A: Johnny Appleseed (John Chapman)

Card: Plants and Animals
Q: What plant is associated with March 17?
A: Shamrock [four-leaf clover is also acceptable]

Card: Plants and Animals
Q: What is the name of the family of plants that includes peas, clover, beans, and peanuts?
A: Legumes

Card: Plants and Animals
Q: What is the name of the day celebrated on March 24?
A: Agriculture Day

Card: Inventors and Inventions
Q: Name the city that became the first to be lit by electric lights on March 24, 1880.
A: Wabash, Indiana

April Questions and Answers

Card: Plants and Animals

Q: All of the following birds, except one, are endangered. Name the one that is not an endangered species: black-capped vireo; red-cockaded woodpecker; whooping crane; red-winged blackbird.
A: Red-winged blackbird

Card: Miscellaneous

Q: What Spanish explorer landed in Florida in 1513?
A: Juan Ponce de Leon

Card: Plants and Animals

Q: What is the name of the gas needed by animals in respiration (breathing, inhaling)?
A: Oxygen

Card: Plants and Animals

Q: What is the name of the gas exhaled during respiration in animals?
A: Carbon dioxide

Card: Plants and Animals

Q: What is the name of the small holes found in the undersides of leaves? Carbon dioxide enters through them and oxygen exits through them.
A: Stomata

Card: Health and Nutrition

Q: What organ of respiration is found in mammals but not in fish?
A: Lungs

Card: Miscellaneous

Q: What word means "careful use and preservation of our natural resources, like plants, animals, water, and soil"?
A: Conservation

Card: Plants and Animals

Q: What day for honoring plants and trees falls on the last Friday in April?
A: Arbor Day

Card: Miscellaneous

Q: What event occurs the first Sunday in April that lasts for six months and affects our telling of time?

A: Change to daylight saving time

Card: Inventors and Inventions

Q: What is the unit of measurement of a lightbulb's use of energy?

A: Watt, wattage

Card: Inventors and Inventions

Q: What is the unit of measurement of a lightbulb's brightness?

A: Lumens

Card: Space and Aviation

Q: What was the name of the famous $1.5 billion space telescope launched with the space shuttle *Discovery* on April 25, 1990?

A: Hubble space telescope

May–June Questions and Answers

Card: Inventors and Inventions

Q: On May 4, 1776, an American went to France carrying an encoded secret message from the American military. What was it written in?

A: Invisible ink

Card: Inventors and Inventions

Q: On May 8, 1886, a pharmacist named John Styth Pemberton invented a syrup in his backyard and sold it to make special drinks. What was this drink?

A: Coca-Cola

Card: Miscellaneous

Q: On May 12, 1880, the founder of modern nursing was born. Who was she?

A: Florence Nightingale

Card: Space and Aviation

Q: On May 14, 1973, the first manned space station was launched. Name it.

A: *Skylab I*

Card: Space and Aviation

Q: Who was the first woman to fly solo across the Atlantic Ocean?

A: Amelia Earhart

Card: Space and Aviation

Q: Who was the first American astronaut to walk in space (*Gemini IV,* June 3, 1965)?

A: Edward White

Card: Space and Aviation

Q: Who was the first American woman to fly in a space shuttle (*Challenger,* June 18, 1983)?

A: Sally Ride

Card: Space and Aviation

Q: Who was the famous pilot who crossed the Atlantic in his plane, *Spirit of St. Louis,* on May 20, 1927?

A: Charles Lindbergh

Card: Space and Aviation

Q: Who were the first two pilots to fly over the North Pole in 1926?

A: Richard Byrd and Floyd Bennett

Card: Miscellaneous

Q: In which U.S. state was the transcontinental railroad completed in 1869?

A: Utah

Card: Inventors and Inventions

Q: Who successfully tested the first car in Detroit in 1896?

A: Henry Ford

Card: Space and Aviation

Q: What is the name for the first day of summer?

A: Summer solstice

Card: Space and Aviation

Q: What is the shape of the path of Earth's revolution around the sun?

A: An ellipse

Card: Miscellaneous

Q: A record-high June temperature was set in Death Valley, California, on June 25, 2006. What was the temperature?

A: 125°F

Appendix 6
Reproducible Charts and Forms

MONTHLY STUDENT PROGRESS CHART

Student's Name: _____

Month: _____

#	Activity	(✓) Complete	Date Completed

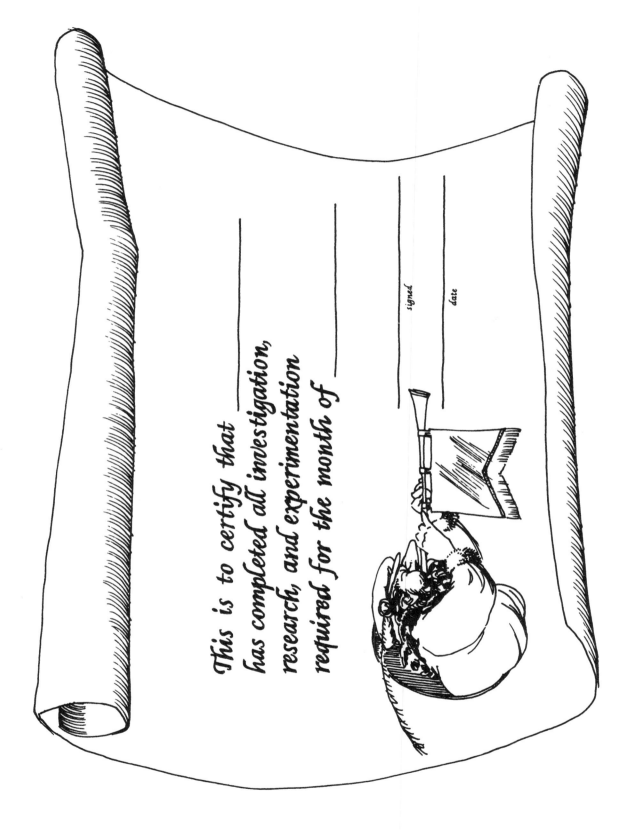

This is to certify that

_____

has completed all investigation,
research, and experimentation
required for the month of

_____

signed

date

Dear Parents

_____

_____

_____

_____

_____

_____

_____

_____

_____

Name: _____

Date: _____

SCIENCE MINI-REPORT

Pick an event or person you've studied this month and write a mini-report. In the space marked BIBLIOGRAPHY list 3 sources (books, magazines, videos) you used in your research.

BIBLIOGRAPHY

1.

2.

3.

Name: _____

Date: _____

SCIENCE REPORT PLAQUE

IN HONOR OF

_____

Write the name of the person you chose

Major Contributions to Science:

_____

_____

_____

_____

Personal Life:

_____

_____

_____

In your own words, how did this person's contribution change the course of history? (Write your answer on the back.)

Name _____
Date _____

SCIENCE CURRENT EVENTS

Reporter's name _____
Date of event _____
Describe what happened _____
_____
_____
_____
_____
_____

Attach a newspaper article about this event to the
back of this report.
Why is this event "noteworthy"? _____
_____
_____
_____

Make two
science
trivia cards
based on
your findings.

Name _____ Date _____

WHO'S WHO IN SCIENCE

Famous people we recognize this month:

Name: _____ Date: _____

Write a biographical sketch of a person you learned about this month. Read and find out about the most significant events in this person's life. Then describe these events in your own words on the lines provided. Choose one of the events and illustrate it within the picture frame.

_____

_____

_____

_____

_____

_____

_____

_____

_____

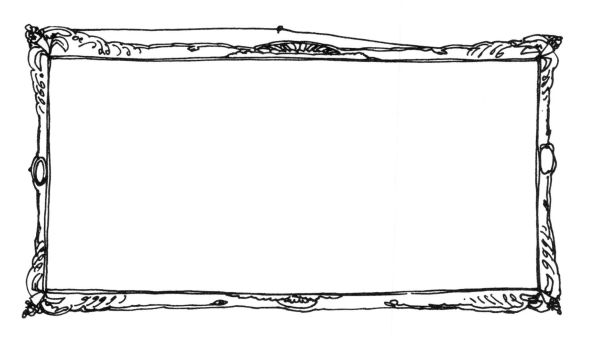

SCIENCE
VOCABULARY WORDS

While you read about the people and events that changed the history of science this month, you may come across words you will not understand. Write those words below and then look them up. Write the definition next to each word.

_____
_____
_____
_____
_____
_____
_____
_____
_____
_____
_____
_____

Other Books of Interest

Hands-On Earth Science Activities For Grades K–6, Second Edition

Marvin N. Tolman, Ed.D.

Paper / 464 pages / ISBN: 0-7879-7866-3
www.josseybass.com

"The Hands-On *books are an awesome resource that has enhanced my science units. Every activity has easy step-by-step instructions, a materials list, and teacher information. My students and I love the activities."*—Patti W. Seeholzer, third-grade teacher, River Heights Elementary School, Utah, and winner of the 2002 Presidential Award for Excellence in Science Teaching

This second edition of Marvin N. Tolman's bestselling book offers compelling activities that help teach students thinking and reasoning skills along with basic science concepts and facts. The book's activities follow the discovery/inquiry approach and encourage students to analyze, synthesize, and infer based on their own hands-on experiences. The updated edition includes an expanded "Teacher Information" section for many of the activities; enhanced user friendliness; inquiry-based models; and increased emphasis on cooperative learning, writing, and collaboration in the classroom. Projects use materials easily found around the classroom or home, link activities to national science standards, and include other new material. Many of the activities could become great science fair projects.

The study of earth science at the elementary school level includes more than 160 easy-to-use, hands-on activities in the following areas:

- Air
- Water
- Weather
- The Earth (mapping, topography, rocks, minerals, and earthquakes)
- Ecology
- Above the Earth (gravity and flight)
- Beyond the Earth (celestial bodies)

Marvin N. Tolman, Ed.D., is a popular presenter at national meetings of science teachers, contributes to academic journals, reviews science education materials, and edits textbook and journal series. Currently, he is professor of teacher education at Brigham Young University and author of the popular *Hands-On Science* series from Jossey-Bass.

Other Books of Interest

Science Sleuths:
60 Forensic Activities to Develop Critical Thinking and Inquiry Skills, Grades 4–8

Pam Walker and Elaine Wood

Paper / 360 pages / ISBN: 0-7879-7435-8

www.josseybass.com

"*Science Sleuths is a great book for the teacher who hopes to engage middle school students in science investigations that build upon high-interest topics related to mystery, clues, and intrigue.*"—Dr. Gail H. Marshall, Ed. D., assistant professor, College of Education, University of West Georgia

Science Sleuths is an easy-to-use guide that will help you teach students how to unravel forensic science mysteries while improving their critical thinking skills. What your students won't realize is that by solving these mysteries they are engaging in problem solving, application, and synthesis. The activities and experiments in *Science Sleuths* vary widely, covering topics that range from techniques for sharpening observation skills to recipes for extracting DNA, and they can all be completed without specialized lab equipment. By putting the focus on skills related to critical thinking, the book helps students

- Identify questions that can be answered through scientific investigation
- Collect and analyze data
- Explain scientific concepts and make predictions
- Make logical deductions and develop explanations based on evidence
- Share findings with others clearly and logically
- Integrate math and writing skills with science

Each chapter in this helpful teaching aid contains eight in-class experiments and activities plus two homework assignments that will engage the interest of young, budding scientists. The activities all include a teacher briefing section, clear activity preparation steps (with lists of materials needed), background information to familiarize students with the topic, detailed procedure descriptions, and conclusion questions.

Pam Walker, M.Ed., has twenty-three years of experience in teaching science and was named 2007 Georgia Teacher of the Year.

Elaine Wood, M.S., has spent thirteen years teaching science. Both Walker and Wood teach science in Douglasville, Georgia. They are coauthors of several resource books, including *Hands-On General Science Activities with Real-Life Applications*, *Crime Scene Investigations: Real-Life Science Labs for Grades 6–12*; and *Crime Scene Investigations*: *Real-Life Science Activities for Elementary Grades*.

Other Books of Interest

Family Science
Activities, Projects, and Games That Get Everyone Excited About Science

Sandra Markle

Paper / 282 pages / ISBN: 0-471-65197-4
www.josseybass.com

Family Science is a great book for extending the classroom science lessons to home participation. Divided into lively, thematic chapters that arrange the activities by age level, each step-by-step experiment lets parents mentor their children as they discover the world around them and practice key problem-solving skills. From biology and chemistry to earth science and physics, they'll tackle investigations, experiments, expeditions, and competitions guaranteed to bring out everyone's inner scientist. Best of all, each activity can be completed with everyday items found around the house, so they can get started right away!

Here's what's inside:

- Create a Juicy T-Shirt
- Launch Spaghetti Rockets
- Go on a Night Safari
- Bake Foam You Can Eat
- Turn Glue into Glubber
- Make Your Own Marshmallows
- Grow a Room
- Make Animal Splits
- Whip Up Your Own Chalk
- Blow Super Soap Bubbles
- Walk the Plank
- And Much More!

Sandra Markle is the award-winning author of more than seventy science books for children and educators. She's developed science TV specials for CNN and PBS, developed a science education website for the National Science Foundation, and written for many magazines, including Disney's *FamilyFun*. Markle is also a nationally known science education consultant who frequently speaks at workshops and conventions and visits schools, presenting hands-on science programs for children.

Other Books of Interest

Hands-On Science Mysteries Grades 3–6

Standards-Based Inquiry Investigation

James Robert Taris and Louis James Taris, Ed.D.

Paper / 297 pages / ISBN: 0-471-69760-5

www.josseybass.com

"In this brand new collection, Louis and James Taris have called upon science's most curious mysteries to provide food for critical thinking skills. Hands-On Science Mysteries is just what students and teachers need to connect science to real-world situations by becoming involved in the process of hands-on experimentation."—Professor C. David Luther, Graduate School of Education, Cambridge College

Hands-On Science Mysteries for Grades 3–6 is an exciting collection of lab-based programs that show students how to examine mysterious phenomena scientifically! Each lab is filled with intriguing mysteries and provocative exercises that will challenge students to develop problem solving and critical thinking skills.

In *Hands-On Science Mysteries for Grades 3–6*, the authors connect science to real-world situations by investigating actual mysteries and phenomena, such as the strange heads on Easter Island, the ghost ship *Mary Celeste*, and the "Dancing Stones" of Death Valley. The labs encourage the development of science inquiry, in which students will observe, take notes, make diagrams, interpret data, and arrive at solutions.

Static electricity, simple machines, density, optics, combustion, the use of science equipment, states of matter, and heat are just a sampling of the basic science concepts and skills, designed to reflect the National Science Standards, that students will learn when conducting these fascinating experiments. Most of the labs use common items found in the classroom or at home.

James Robert Taris and **Louis James Taris, Ed.D.,** are teachers, curriculum developers, and published authors with over fifty years collectively of experience in science education. James is currently a middle school and high school teacher in Massachusetts, and Dr. Louis is a former professor of teacher training at Bridgewater State College and a former school superintendent.